RAMBLES BEYOND RAILWAYS
IN DEVON

RAMBLES *beyond* RAILWAYS *in* DEVON

Dennis Needham

EX LIBRIS PRESS

Published in 1995 by
EX LIBRIS PRESS
1 The Shambles
Bradford on Avon
Wiltshire

Design and typesetting by Ex Libris Press

Cover printed by Shires Press, Trowbridge
Printed and bound in Britain by
Cromwell Press, Broughton Gifford, Wiltshire

ISBN0 948578 73 4

By the same Author:

Canal Walks : Volume 1: North (Cicerone)
Best Pub Walks in North Devon (Sigma)

For Nigel, a lifetime lover of railways, now discovering walking.

With apologies to Wilkie Collins whose book, Rambles Beyond
Railways, or Notes in Cornwall taken a-foot, *published in 1851,
inspired the editor to recycle Mr Collins' evocative title in the
present work.*

CONTENTS

Preface

Most people who enjoy walking at least pay lip service to 'green' issues, and how to square the transport circle exercises all our minds at some time. But a nation grown accustomed to freedom of movement will not give up that pleasure, still only a generation old, without a fight. How then to reconcile a desire to travel with the need to cut down on car use. Public transport is the only obvious answer.

But this is a generally unpopular way to travel. The perception of buses that run only in convoys and trains adhering more to horoscope than timetable is unfair and outdated. We all – the present author included – have berated British Rail for stunning examples of ineptitude. They are still the butt of every comedian who can always be guaranteed a laugh if he mentions 'leaves on the rails' in autumn, or 'the wrong kind of snow' in winter. But how many, hand on heart (London commuters excepted), can say that today's train service is bad? Are carriages dirty? Do trains run late? Are the staff surly and uninterested? Is it expensive?

The answer, unless you are singularly unfortunate, is a resounding *No*. During the research for these walks, a whole bunch of preconceived ideas were dashed. I travelled slightly in excess of 2,000 miles. Many of the services were Regional Railway Wales and West trains, some InterCity, and a few belonged to South West Trains. The only litter I experienced was from passengers earlier in the journey. Most of the carriage windows were clean in the morning, occasionally mud-spattered later in the day. Every single member of staff with whom I had any contact was polite and helpful. Value for money? Absolutely unbeatable. Three weeks travel on a Devon Regional Rover ticket cost me £4.30 a day or 4.5p per mile. My small car costs almost 6p per mile just for petrol. I had no parking fees, no traffic jams and no breathalyser.

And the schedules? Well, I used 74 different trains in total. One was 20 minutes late, three were around ten minutes late, and, apart from eight others, every single one was within two minutes of the expected arrival time. The other eight? They were *early*. Was I lucky?

Were the railways trying to impress me? I can only speak as I find, and my few weeks intimate acquaintance with the iron road turned me from neutral to very pro-rail. How the privatisation measures currently being introduced will affect things remains to be seen. Cutting through all the political dogma, I am hopeful. The most telling comment on this subject came from a guard on a Regional Rail service to Barnstaple. Talking about track repairs on the main line that weekend, he was mainly concerned as to how they would affect the performance figures of 'his' company. Another used 'we' when taking about the Regional Railways service. There is a nascent sense of belonging in some of the staff. Were that sentiment reflected throughout, the railways would have a very secure future.

Dennis Needham
June 1995

Introduction

Rambles Beyond Railways is a collection of walks in Devon with train travel as the theme. That said, it is not targeted exclusively at rail users. Almost a third of the 20 walks are circular. If you are mindful, drive to the station, park your car and enjoy the walk. Or, from the station, take a one-way walk and use the train for the short return journey.

It was, however, envisaged as a means of seeing Devon without the unremitting hard work of driving. And hard work it surely is. Anyone who has more than a passing acquaintance with the county knows that narrow high-banked lanes are the norm, motorways a rarity. It also almost entirely eliminates the problems of parking, and allows visits to Torbay free of the car. Anyone who has tried to drive in this area during the season will know what a blessed relief that is. The secret of travel is a Regional Rover ticket; what a shame so few people know of this gem.

For a very reasonable sum of money, you can buy travel for three days in seven, or for a full week. The concept behind walking with a travelling friend like this is that you can base yourself in most parts of Devon without being too far from a railway station. From your selected base – which can change in the week if you choose – you travel anywhere in the county. Plan your journey in advance, or take spur-of-the-moment decisions as the mood strikes you. Although the Devon rail network was decimated by Beeching, as was the rest of the country, there are still 47 stations in use.

From out of a train window, the whole scene is transformed. No traffic jams or road works to worry about. A relaxing journey with food and drink if you want. Some stations are in the centre of towns or cities, but Devon is not a county of huge settlements. There are only two cities, Plymouth with half a million inhabitants is the largest; the next – Exeter – doesn't even reach six figures. Mostly, you will de-train directly into the country, or within a few minutes walk thereof. From each station, carefully researched directions will take you on a most pleasing route to the finish point – whether that is back at the start, or another station. There is a wide mix of walks with country, town, farm lane and muddy field. Some fit the 'dry shoe' category. These can be confidently undertaken in lightweight footwear without any problem.

There are also two city walks: if you think that a walk must be green fields to be interesting, disabuse yourself of that idea on Walk 2 in Plymouth. At the start of each description is a small block of facts, together with a very brief outline of what to expect. From this information you can pick out the walks with very steep hills – plenty of those in Devon – and a note of any problems during the walk.

Details of the various attractions encountered en-route are included. Any details concerning opening hours are current at the time of writing. Telephone numbers are included where possible, and local Tourist Information Offices (TIC's) are usually able to help with current information.

Following this, walking instructions are indented and highlighted with a vertical double line, with further information included in full page as encountered.

And, in case the joys of whizzing unfettered around the countryside on fast modern trains begin to pall, there is further variety. Devon is host to two preserved railway lines. Both these are utilised in the walks. From the air-conditioned comfort of the main line, step back in history as old locomotives wreathed in steam and smoke haul vintage carriages through breathtakingly beautiful scenery. It's now over a quarter of a century since these behemoths of another more relaxed age were taken out of service, but their fascination for boys (and girls) from the cradle to Queen's telegram never seems to pall. One very slight difficulty in Devon is that, acre for acre, it has one of the smallest number of public footpaths in the country. The historical reason for this is that there were so many small roads and lanes that trudging across fields was never greatly needed. And there is a bonus here. When roads were adopted by the council and made up, there were so many that a proportion of them were surplus to requirements and left alone. Over the years these have acquired the appellation 'Green Lane', are still unpaved, but available to pedestrians. Several of these will be used during the course of this book.

For the rest, some walks use the narrow country lanes. On many of these you can walk all day and not see a car. Tractors and combine harvesters, yes; even a herd of cows being taken in for milking. But generally, these small lanes are as peaceful as the rest of the county, once you get away from the holidaymakers who stick to very predictable routes. With an odd exception, you will find these walks keeping you very close to nature and the glories of this wonderful mix of scenery which is the county of Devon.

For information on a Rail Rover ticket, pick up a leaflet at your nearest station or call 0181 986 1010 for a copy.

The Railways of Devon

One name stands out above all others when the history of Devon's railways is written: Isambard Kingdom Brunel. His was the engineering genius that built the Saltash Bridge (seen from the train en route to Walk 1) and surveyed, planned and built many of the other lines in the county. He was also a passionate advocate of the 7 feet gauge which was to cause continual conflict with other companies who adopted the 'narrow' Stephenson gauge of 4 feet 8.5 inches. This was never really resolved in Brunel's time, but The Great Western Railway, realising that it had lost the battle of the gauges, converted to narrow in 1892 which then became 'standard'.

But railways were relatively late on the scene here. Small private ones such as the Haytor Granite Railway (see Walk 7) were in use early in the 19th century, but the main thrust of railway expansion did not sunder the peace of the region until 1 May 1844. Then a train from London rolled into Exeter just after noon, having completed the journey of almost 200 miles in five hours, a staggering achievement in that era. The Bristol and Exeter Railway Company built the line and operated it until 1876 when they sold out to the GWR.

The next task was to extend to Plymouth, and here Brunel made one of his few major errors. Because of the severe gradients between the two cities, he cast around for alternative forms of power. An atmospheric system was chosen·that used air pressure as the propelling force. Abject failure was the result. The leather-lined valves refused to stay airtight, succumbing to the joint attack of rats and salt-laden air.

Plymouth was duly reached in 1848 with steam locomotives actually coping very well on the adverse gradients. From then, expansion was measured rather than dramatic. A line to Crediton had been built in 1847 to 'narrow' gauge, and the resultant clash came at Cowley Bridge, just outside Exeter, where their line met the B & E's

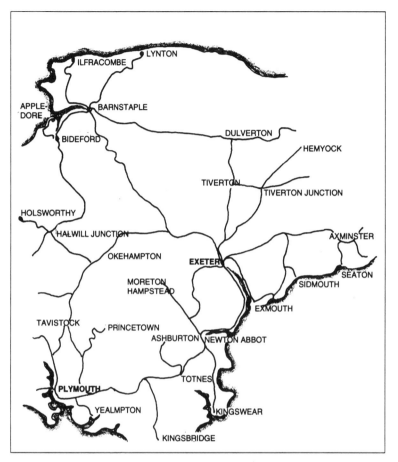

Devonian Passenger Railways earlier this century

broad gauge. It then remained unused until a compromise was reached four years later that saw dual-gauge track in use.

Extensions to Barnstaple and Torbay were completed in the 1850s and the London and South Western Railway brought their 'narrow' gauge track from London to Exeter via Salisbury in 1860. Then the battle of the gauges was effectively joined.

Their expansion was mainly to the north of the county, although they also built a line from Exeter to Plymouth around the north side of Dartmoor through Okehampton which opened in 1890. In later –

Southern Railway – years, these north Devon – and Cornwall – lines became known as the 'Withered Arm', so far were they from head office at London's Waterloo station.

One line of particular interest to enthusiasts of the day was the Lynton and Barnstaple line. This was a genuine narrow gauge, built with 1 foot 11.5 inch track which opened up the resort of Lynton to tourists. But it was mainly seasonal traffic; there were simply not enough locals to generate the trade needed to sustain it. The last train ran in 1935.

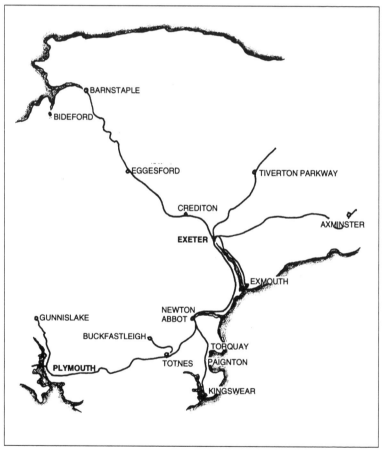

Devonian passenger railways today.

Over the next 30 years, several branch lines and smaller stations in the county saw their final train services. The line toPrincetown, serving the nearby Dartmoor prison was one sadly missed, particularly in winter when the railway kept going long after roads became impassable. The Ashburton branch closed to passenger traffic in 1958 although a preservation society retained much of this line (see Walk 4). But a sword of Damoclesian proportions was hanging over the national railway system.

March 1963 saw the publication of a report by the then Chairman of British Railways, Dr. Richard Beeching. Entitled 'The Reshaping of British Railways,' it sought closure of huge tracts of non-profitable lines and stations, and Devon suffered along with the rest of the country. Not only were branch lines doomed, but main lines as well. From Taunton to Barnstaple along the edge of Exmoor was a dramatic line that disappeared completely, as did the route from Exeter to Plymouth via Okehampton. One short length of this survives today linking the old Callington (Cornwall) branch – now open only as far as Gunnislake – with Plymouth (see Walk 1). The 'withered arm' became a finger as only the Exeter to Barnstaple service survived.

But there are still 165 miles remaining and there to be enjoyed. The Waterloo to Exeter line is open – albeit as a semi–fast, single track. Any further closures seem very unlikely given the continuing pressure for improved public transport. Most of the rolling stock seems modern and reliable, although this can be something of an illusion. The InterCity 125s which whizz along the main Devon line will soon be entering their third decade of service. Locomotive-hauled trains are the exception, and the diesel units are all under ten years old, some well under.

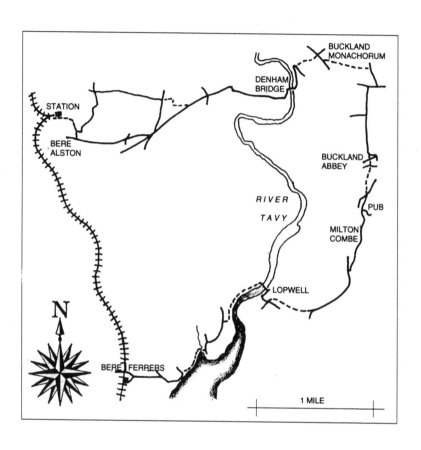

Walk 1
Bere Ferrers to Bere Alston

This is the most westerly walk in the book. It takes in the delightful Tavy valley and offers so much interest and beauty it would be hard to find a better start.

Starting Station: Bere Ferrers on the Plymouth to Gunnislake service
Distance: 9.5 miles
Finishing Station: Bere Alston
Map: 201
TIC: Island House, 9 The Barbican, Plymouth, Devon PL1 2LS; Tel 01752 264849
Problems: Hills. There is virtually nothing on the level and includes one mile of continuous climb which starts off at 1 in 4. It does ease later: to 1 in 8!

The railway on which this walk relies is a remnant of an earlier age: a branch line. It was originally part of the London and South Western Railway's line from Exeter to Plymouth around the north edge of Dartmoor, being closed as a through route on 5 May 1968. But, somehow, the branch from Bere Alston to Callington managed to evade the axe; only the furthest 5 miles falling: literally. They were closed mainly because of mining subsidence, and the line now terminates at Gunnislake. And, to complete the link, the remainder of the track from Bere Alston to Plymouth is used, although re–routing in the latter city allowed the LSWR station at Friary to be closed.

The station at Bere Ferrers is something of an anomoly. The buildings have been sold, and the new owner is a railway enthusiast. A small siding to the south of the platform houses a few ancient coaches, in the process of being renovated, and the house has old station signs adorning the walls. Fine: except that they are in the tangerine colours adopted by the North Eastern region of BR after nationalisation in 1948, and never within 300 miles of this station.

Leave the station along the approach road and bear right at the end into the village. Follow the road to the bottom and turn right, opposite Bere Ferrers Social Club. This leads down to the edge of the Tavy estuary and the road bears left. After a few yards, hard by the derestriction signs, a path leads off to the right along the shore in front of a row of houses.

After some 200 yards, the track bears to the left over a stile, following a Public Footpath sign, still keeping close to the water's edge but a little way above it. This path eventually drops down to water level again and heads towards a flat bridge and ford across an arm of the river. Cross this, and a few yards further along is a left turn into a semi-paved track. This leads very soon to a road; turn right, up the first hill.

As the gradient starts to ease a little, there is a right turn into a green lane. Take this and follow it steeply downhill, through beautiful woodland, back down to the water's edge. Here, a narrow causeway takes the walk over the river with a waterfall a few feet to the left. This is man-made; Lopwell Dam has a salmon ladder at the far corner, and marks the upper limit of the tide.

Turn right and pick up a road. Walk back down the river, over a cattle grid and then uphill as the road leaves the water's edge. Cross the second cattle grid and turn left, through a gate, into woodland. This track continues the climb until it meets a paved road. Turn left and follow the road. This eventually drops down into a valley and, as it starts to climb out the other side, take the right fork for Milton Combe. Follow the road through a very pretty village with a stream alongside the road. At the far end, this develops into yet another steep hill.

Milton Combe is everything a Devon village should be. There are cob and thatch cottages, a tiny Church of the Holy Spirit, and a pub. The latter is called The Who'd Have Thought It, and is a 16th century free house. The story is told that, many years ago, the only alcohol to be bought in the village was at an alehouse across the way from this pub, then just a house. Eventually, it was decided that spirits should be available and applications to sell them were invited. This house applied, and to everyone's astonishment, was granted the licence. Who'd Have Thought It started as an opinion, and was adopted as a name.

As a refreshment stop, it's ideally placed. There is a fine range of ales and cider on draught, and good quality food is served. It's also quite well placed in the context of this walk, being just over a third of the way along.

The Who'd Have Thought It Inn.

At the top of the hill, cross the road and over a stone stile into a small enclosure. Walk alongside the fence, and at the far end is another stile into a field. To the right is what appears to be a turning circle for 'buses.

Here, in deepest Devon, is scarcely the place one would expect to see this sort of construction, awaiting 'that monarch of the road, observer of the Highway Code, that big six-wheeler, scarlet-painted, diesel-engined, 97 horsepower omnibus' so beloved of Flanders and Swann.

Cross this field, over a lane into another field and, at the far end, a stile gives access to another lane. Here, turn left to visit Buckland Abbey.

This is English history at its finest. Founded in 1287 as a Cistercian Abbey, it was sold on the Dissolution to Sir Richard Grenville. He demolished many of the original buildings and converted the abbey church into a mansion. In 1581 Sir Francis Drake became the owner, and was his home whenever he was in England.

Now owned by the National Trust, the house has exhibitions and furnished rooms in the style of that exciting period in history. In the grounds, it is possible to see remains of other monastic buildings and a superb tithe barn. Details of opening times from 01822 853607.

To continue the walk, carry straight on for a few yards until another entrance to the Abbey crosses. Here, on the right is a metal kissing gate. Pass through it and walk alongside the lane. At the far end is another gate which leads to a road. Cross this, through another gate and at the top turn left along the road.

Walk along this road towards Buckland Monachorum. At the T-junction turn right and take the second left into the village. On the left hand side is a Post Office, and at the corner of the building is a footpath, but before taking it, examine the village.

The Drake Manor pub is a delightful old building, very long and serving good food and ales. Next door, the parish church of St. Andrew, is a fine example of Perpendicular Gothic architecture. Built entirely of granite it is high-roofed and quite large considering the size of this village, there are several memories of Drake to be found here. A Saxon font stands just inside the entrance to the left, being rediscovered during some work on the foundations in 1857.

The footpath leads into a road. Walk along this, staying on the right hand side and at the end, on the right, is another Public Footpath sign pointing half right. After a few yards, this enters a field. Keep well to the left, towards a gateway. Pass through this and turn right along a lane beside farm buildings. Keep in a straight line, ignoring an apparently major turn to the right. At the end of the next field, a stile gives access into a lane; turn right.

Only a few yards along, a road junction is reached. At this point, there is a driveway to the left. Walk up it, keeping an eye open for a single concrete gatepost on the left. Just a few paces past this, almost hidden in the undergrowth, is a narrow pathway to the left, a yellow waymark arrow eventually visible. The main drive heads right into the grounds of a house. If you arrive there, you've missed the turn.

This path crosses a series of fields, eventually reaching a road on the apex of a hairpin bend. Turn right, down the hill. Turn right at the bridge to cross the Tavy again and up the hill beyond. This is the 1 in 4. After almost a mile, there is an alternative route, following a Public Footpath sign to the right.

This is detailed at the foot of this Walk. It rejoins the main walk at *.

A busier road arrives from the right to join the walk. Cross over, and walk to the left for a few yards before taking another quiet lane to the right. After almost a mile, by which time the road has entered Bere Alston, there is a right turn with a width restriction for vehicles. 100 yards along the road turns sharp right and on the left is an entrance to a couple of fields.*

Between the two, a few yards off the road surface is a narrow path, fenced each side, leaving half left and downhill. This is the walk. It reaches a roughly surfaced lane; turn left and immediately there is a choice of routes. The one straight across leads to Bere Alston station.

ALTERNATIVE ROUTE. Follow the footpath until it joins a road. Across, but the the left, another lane leads away. Walk along here and down the hill, across a crossroads and over the old Exeter to Plymouth railway and turn very sharply left with the road, signposted Bere Alston. Up the hill, back over the railway and the road reaches the sharp bend and rejoins the main walk at *).

A Regional Railways Gunnislake to Plymouth service arrives at Bere Alston in wintry evening sunshine.

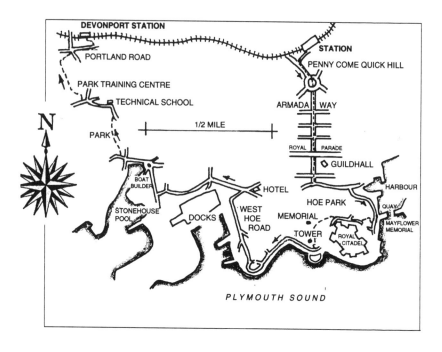

Walk 2
Plymouth to Devonport

This is unashamedly a city walk: but what a walk. Anyone with the slightest knowledge of our naval past cannot fail to find this short stroll absorbing. Sir Francis Drake, The Pilgrim Fathers, Sir Joshua Reynolds; all have intimate connection with Plymouth. And, as this is a city walk, one with far more than its share of interest and time-consuming activities, allow more time than usual for a walk of just four miles.

> **Starting Station:** Plymouth
> **Distance:** 4 miles
> **Finishing Station:** Devonport
> **Map:** 201. The Geographia A to Z Street Plan of Plymouth is a useful – if occasionally unwieldy – adjunct.
> **TIC:** 9 The Barbican, Plymouth, Devon PL1 2LS; Tel 01752 264849

Turn right on leaving the station and left at the main road, Penny-come-Quick Hill. On reaching the huge traffic island, take the underpass marked for pedestrians which leads into the traffic-free Armada Way.

There is literally everything you could want in this part of the city. One section has nothing but banks and building societies on each side. There is a Sainsbury's, plenty of food, and a pub or two. This whole area has a modernity about it, with scarcely an old building remaining. This owes nothing to insensitive planners; all to that greatest of all demolition experts: Adolf Hitler. It was his Luftwaffe that pasted the city in 1941, attempting to eliminate the naval facilities. What he did achieve was the destruction of 20,000 buildings which included over 100 pubs and hotels, 40 churches, 24 schools and eight cinemas. Over a thousand people died and five thousand were injured during the Blitz which lasted from 1940 to 1943. For its size, Plymouth received more bomb damage that almost any other British city.

21

Under the road bridge – Royal Parade, noting The Guildhall on the left, also rebuilt after the war, across Princess Street with its fountain in San Sebastian Square, heading generally towards the Moat House Hotel, and turn left at Notte Street, opposite a huge ship's anchor.

This passage under the road forms the base for a mural, stretching all down one side and back up the other. It traces the history of this famous city from Henry VII to The Falkland Task Force which left here in 1982.

The anchor, an enormous monument to Plymouth's naval connections came from *HMS Ark Royal*, and was presented to the city by the Admiralty Board in 1980.

Continue along Notte Street, but you can make a short diversion by turning first left into Finewell Street and then right into the Square and right again into Andrew Street to regain the main road.

This short detour reveals a wealth of buildings, some dating back to 1498. This is the ancient heart of Plymouth, known as Sutton Place. The parish church, St. Andrew, was another victim of the war, although the tower was saved, and is original.

Walk along Notte Street until you reach the delightfully different Notte Inn on the left. Opposite, the walk turns right into Southside Street and leads to the old Fish Quay and the historic Pier.

This area, once the heart of Plymouth's harbour was, within living memory, a rather quiet corner of the city. Now, it's a bright cheerful place and a very tourist-based economy, but with history leaping out of every nook and cranny. These are actually the streets down which Sir Francis Drake and Sir Walter Raleigh strode. There is the home of Plymouth Dry Gin, a distillery owned by Coates that is now open to visitors. The Palace Vaults, a little further along, was the repository for prizes taken by the navy during the Napoleonic wars.

That there is so much genuine history still left to see in Plymouth is due to some very far-seeing citizens. When other cities were tearing down their old buildings, a local committee was devising ways to save Plymouth. As far back as 1929, The Elizabethan House was saved, and the interior now shows how people of that period lived.

Across the road is Island House, where some of the 162 Pilgrim Fathers are believed to have spent their last night on English soil, before the *Mayflower* left for the New World on 6 September 1620. The Pier from which their voyage started also saw many other famous arrivals and departures. Some of them are commemorated by plaques on the quay.

Walk up the hill for a few yards and take a flight of steps on the right. At the top, turn back towards the Barbican, to the right of The Commercial Inn, and to the remains of The Castle.

This was a late 14th century building, constructed to defend Sutton Harbour. Most of it was demolished in the mid-17th century; only the tower and part of a wall remain.

Turn left and walk under the passage formed by new housing overhead which leads into Lambhay hill, passing The Fishermans Arms, selling the excellent St. Austell Ales. Bear right and cross the road to walk alongside The Citadel. Pass the main gates and turn left at the end, still keeping the grey wall to your immediate left. Past the guarded entrance, cross the road and climb the steps to the obelisk there.

A star-shaped fortress, The Citadel was built between 1666 and 1675. Still run by the military, it is currently home to 29 Commando, Royal Artillery. There are tours available, but only as part of a Guided Tour, starting from the Dome daily at 12noon and 2pm from 1May to 30 September.
The obelisk is erected to the memory of the officers, non-commissioned officers and men of the Gloucestershire, Somersetshire and Devonshire regiments who fell in the Boer War 1899 to 1902.

Take the path heading half right that leads towards the lighthouse. Cross The Hoe, walk down to the road below and turn right. To the south is the famed Plymouth Sound where there is usually a warship or two at anchor. The Breakwater and Drake's Island can also be seen.

Smeaton's Tower was originally built by that great engineer on the Eddystone Rocks in 1759, and was to set the standard of lighthouse construction for many years. Its base eventually cracked, and it was re-erected here in 1882. Drake's famous game of Bowls was played on The Hoe and two memorials erected in the 1880s mark the site of this event.
The Plymouth Dome houses some wonderful exhibitions; not only concerning the city's past, although Drake and company are well represented. The Dome itself offers a unique view out to sea, with radar, remote

television, and touch screen computers to identify shipping in the Sound. Hi-tech wizardry for all.

The Breakwater was started in 1812 and not finished until 1840. It took 4.5 million tons of limestone rock to complete. There is also a large fort on the top, although this was completed separately.

Drake's Island was once known as St. Nicholas' Island, after the chapel of that name that was demolished in 1548 to make way for military installations. It was once used as a prison and was for many years under the control of the military. Subsequently it saw use as an Adventure Centre, but is currently disused because of the unsafe state of both the boat landing and buildings.

Follow The Hoe around the shoreline, past a series of swimming pools at Tinside and towards West Hoe Pier. Here, there is The Wet Wok Chinese restaurant set into the cliffs, looking out to the Sound. The road then becomes Grand Parade with its elegant, but now somewhat jaded housing with ornate ironwork balconies and copper-capped cupolas. As the road bears to the right, a pathway keeps to the shore. This takes the walk around Eddystone Terrace, eventually returning to the road. Turn left and follow Great Western Road. This leads past the RNLI station and away from the historical fascination into a somewhat more downbeat area in West Hoe Road. There is no shortage of facilities along here (or anywhere else on this walk); a pub, The Frog and Frigate, is one of them.

At the traffic island is an elegant hotel across the road, The Duke of Cornwall. Here, turn sharp left alongside another pub, Sippers.

This odd name has naval connections: surprise! It goes back to the days when the navy issued rum rations to sailors. When some of the ration was saved, it would be offered to another, perhaps as repayment for a debt, or as a token of friendship. This was known as 'sippers.'

This is Millbay Road and, after a few yards, there is a small traffic island. Take the exit that is slightly to the right of straight on; the left one leads into the commercial docks where ferries leave for the continent. The low wall along here gives a good view of the harbour.

At the next crossroads, turn right into Durnford Road and at the bottom, where the Brewery Taps pub is on the right, turn left.

This is a causeway over the end of Stonehouse Pool and is home to boatbuilders, one of whom turns out some rather swish cabin cruisers. Over this bridge, there is a crossroads. On the right is a grassed area with a path leading off diagonally. This is the walk.

When this path meets another one, bear right, and then, almost immediately left to return to a road. Turn left, towards a large building with a clock tower, which will turn out to be Devonport Municipal Science and Technical School.

The sports fields to the left has a macabre story to tell. It was around here that more than a thousand victims of cholera were buried in a mass grave in 1849.

Keep to the left at the next junction, but cross shortly and enter a gateway to the right into Devonport Park Training Centre. Take a left at the first fork after 50 yards and follow this path uphill. The splendid brick building to the left is a retirement home. Where several paths meet, take the left one, staying in front of the building. This passes a gun captured from the Boers.

Yet another memorial to that war, it was erected by the officers and crew of *HMS Doris* in remembrance of shipmates who lost their lives in that campaign. From here is a view over the Naval Dockyards at Devonport. These were located here in preference to Falmouth or Dartmouth in 1696, in response to the need for a western base from which to fight the increasing threat from the French. It became a town in its own right in 1837.

Follow the path around to the right and downhill. This exits the park through a gate alongside a white building, Exmouth Social Club on Exmouth Road. Directly across, by the police station, is Portland Road. At the end of there, turn left, and the entrance to Devonport station is a few yards along on the left.

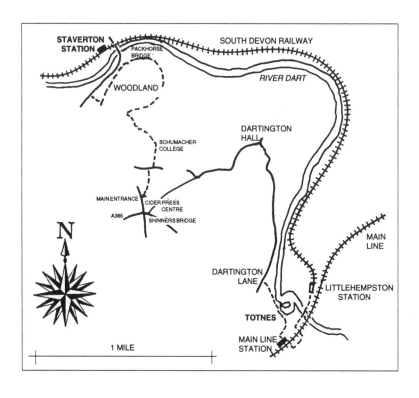

Walk 3
Totnes to Staverton

Although quite a short walk, there really is a mass of interest crammed into it. The huge Dartington Hall with its attached buildings, the Cider Press Centre and a steam railway are all included. And, with the whole walk either on paved or hard-packed surfaces, it qualifies as a 'Clean Shoe Walk'.

Starting Station: Totnes
Distance: 4.5 miles
Finishing Station: Staverton
Map: 202
TIC: The Plains, Totnes, Devon TQ9 5EJ; Tel 01803 863168
Problems: Full walk only available during operating season of the steam train.

Leave the 'up' platform of Totnes main line station into what appears to be the yard of the Unigate creamery. This is Station Yard, and parallel yellow lines indicate a walkway across to a gate at the far side. This leads into a narrow alley around the back of the factory and to a park. At the entrance, a path to the right is The Devon and Dartmoor Cycle Path; and this walk. Follow the path right alongside the Dart to Dartington Lane, where a right turn takes the walk into the grounds of Dartington Hall. Continue up the road into the main body of buildings.

The full story of Dartington Hall and its development has been told in many learned tomes. Suffice it, today, to skim briefly through the centuries.

The first records go back to the early 1100s when a family called Martin were the owners. When the last of that line died without issue in 1384, the estate was escheated. King Richard II then gave it to his half-brother John Holand – soon to become the Earl of Huntington. Much of what can be seen

27

today dates back to his efforts. The Great Hall is still largely as it was, probably the finest of its type still remaining.

The estate passed through several hands over the centuries, and after the Great War, looked set for dereliction. Some of the house was ruined, the roof from the Great Hall had been removed for safety reasons, and an air of decay pervaded.

Enter Dr. Leonard and Dorothy Elmhirst. They bought the estate in 1925, with the idea of an experiment in self-sufficiency. Thus developed the multitude of activities that is today The Dartington Hall Trust. Education in its widest form, and a centre for artistic development are the more esoteric happenings. As the Trust's work has developed, so it has spread its influence through the county. The Beaford College in mid-Devon is another cultural centre, whilst the famed Dartington Glass factory at Torrington in north Devon was established by the Trust in the 1960s. Makers of superb quality glassware, the factory was opened with the aim of providing employment and teaching skills in rural areas suffering depopulation.

The whole estate is private, but their gardens are always open – albeit not for dogs. When unused, The Great Hall can also be visited. The main entrance is on the left from the road through the estate. The Garden Shop is open from 10.30am to 12.30pm and 1.30pm to 5pm every day in summer, but not Sundays in winter.

The Gardens cover some 25 acres and several well-known landscape designers helped in the planning; Percy Cane and Beatrix Farrand among them. By exploring these gardens and following the Rhododendron Walk into the Hydrangea Walk, to exit the gardens beyond the Pavilion into the lane it is possible to pick up the walk from there at *.

Follow the major road right through the estate grounds and out at the other side*. The road goes downhill before arriving at a fork. Take the left hand road which leads into The Dartington Cider Press Centre.

Cider-making, that most Devonian of crafts, was restarted on this site when the Elmhirsts took over the estate. Sadly, that did not survive, but the buildings here today are thriving in their latest manifestation. As a centre for small retail businesses, you can buy a whole range of articles. Food, pottery, Dartington Crystal, plants and gifts are just a few of the shops open for your delectation. Cranks, the famous vegetarian restaurant, is here, together with toilets and a picnic area. There are often displays by craftsmen, and street theatre type of entertainment during the summer and at Christmas.

Leaving by the left hand corner, you will arrive at a main road and Shinners Bridge. Turn right towards the main entrance and on the left a few yards up the A385 is a Post Office and village store. Then retrace your steps to the main entrance. If you do not need the shop, head straight for the main entrance where, on the right, is a Public Footpath sign. At the end of this path, turn right into the lane and take the first left following the sign towards 'Craft Education Centre.'

Another part of the Dartington complex, Schumacher College was established in 1991 in the grounds and house of the Old Postern. Named after the author of *Small is Beautiful*, it differs from conventional education in that it aims to interweave four strands of exploration: deep intellectual study, a strong sense of community, time for quietness and meditation and expressive and creative activities. As a model for the 21st century it seeks to motivate and integrate `head', `hands' and `heart'.

This driveway eventually leads into a narrow path which heads towards woodland along a concrete path. As this path proceeds uphill, it eventually bisects a track. Turn right and follow this path through the trees. It swings to the left around a hill, passes a gate which exits onto a road, but is not an official path, and uphill again to a crossing. Turn right to the road and right again, back down the hill, past the gate you saw recently, and left over the packhorse bridge. Take care here, it is barely wide enough for cars; use the refuges provided.

Cross the railway line and turn left to gain access to Staverton station on the South Devon Railway.

Staverton bridge dates back to 1413 when it was built to replace one destroyed in a flood. Salmon run up the river in season. The village itself is over half a mile to the east and does not figure in the walk, although it can be seen from the train window.

The station is a gem. Still much as it was when it was first opened in 1872, it has won awards for the best preserved railway station. There is no electricity – and never was; all the lamps were oil-lit. Known as The Primrose Line, the South Devon Railway has a chequered history. Once the Great Western Railway branch to Ashburton, it was closed before the Beeching cuts of the 1960s, but a team of local businessmen and enthusiasts announced plans in 1962 to reopen it. Thus, The Dart Valley Light Railway came into being. It was conceived essentially as a business proposition, in contrast to other schemes then current which were mainly concerned with preservation of scenic lines, steam locomotives and vintage rolling stock.

Operations restarted in 1960. Sadly, the length from Buckfastleigh to Ashburton had by then been earmarked for road development, and was beyond saving. Thus Buckfastleigh became the terminus. At the south end, connection with the main line station was not an option, so the company eventually built its own almost at the original junction, just a few yards away.

Staverton Bridge.

In 1972, the company took over the Paignton to Kingswear line (see Walk 6). At the end of the 1989 season, after it became clear that the Buckfastleigh operation was losing money, it decided to concentrate its efforts on the Paignton line. The volunteer arm, The Dart Valley Railway Association, acted quickly through that winter, and after frantic efforts, were able to reopen for the 1990 season 'under new management.'

Now the South Devon Railway Trust, the continued operation of this very pretty line seems assured. If you have the time, don't just use the train to return to Totnes. Ride to Buckfastleigh first. There is a fine collection of railway artifacts on display in the museum there, along with the only surviving engine from the Great Western 7 feet gauge days of the last century. The Abbey too is particularly grand. The original was ruined at the Dissolution, but the site was bought in 1882 by French Benedictine monks who have, over the years, rebuilt the abbey. Nationally known for bees and mead, it is another place that should be on every visitors list of Places Not To Miss.

Alight at Littlehempston Riverside station. From there, a footbridge crosses the river Dart. At the end, turn left, under the main line and right to regain Totnes main line station.

One delightful moment to be savoured here is if a main line train passes. The driver, sitting comfortably in his cab and zooming past at a rapid rate of knots, will sound the horn in greeting to the tiny steam train. The frenetic answering shriek from the steam whistle is a touching meeting of two very conflicting technologies that have over the years served the railways well.

Staverton Station on the South Devon Steam Railway.

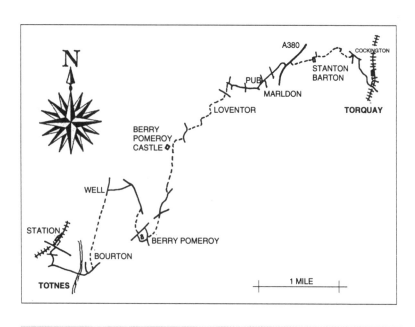

Berry Pomeroy Castle, under the care of English Heritage.

Walk 4
Totnes to Torquay

The contrasts on this walk are many and varied. Historic buildings vie with the best in rolling Devonian scenery in a veritable cornucopia of delight. And a few hills to climb, just to keep you in trim. In fact, there is hardly a level section.

Starting Station: Totnes
Distance: 9.5 miles
Finishing Station: Torquay
Map: 202
TICs: The Plains, Totnes, Devon TQ9 5EJ; Tel 01803 863168
Vaughan Parade, Torquay, Devon TQ2 5JG; Tel 01803 297428

Leave the 'down' platform on the station and turn right. At the top is Station Road. Cross, and opposite is Castle Street (unmarked). Follow this road into a dip, and on reaching a pub called the Globe, as the road turns sharp left, take a narrow alleyway guarded by a metal crush barrier directly across the road which leads up towards the castle. This rejoins Castle Street. Pass under an archway and at the end turn left into High Street.

Totnes is a town of remarkable antiquity, still relatively unsullied by tourists; its list of historical connections most impressive. Prehistoric man, Romans and Saxons all spent time here, evidence of which is on display in the town's museum. Standing out plainly almost as you step from the train are the remains of the castle. Only the keep is left, overlooking the town, but it's in remarkably good condition and under the care of English Heritage. Totnes is the second oldest borough in England, sending its first MP to London in 1295. Two ships, *Crescent* and *Hart*, left Totnes to fight the Spanish Armada.

There is a roll-call of famous people connected with the town. Oliver Cromwell and King Charles I both visited during the Civil War. J M W Turner painted the castle; Charles Babbage, the nineteenth century mathematician and inventor of calculating machines and father of the modern computer lived here; and William Wills, the noted explorer of Australia was also born here. Today, Mary Wesley, prolific author of novels including *The Camomile Lawn* lives close by.

The buildings on Fore Street and High Street are a delight to the eye; some of the merchant houses are over four hundred years old. St Mary's on the left is ornate, with the Guildhall behind, well hidden from view. There was a Benedictine priory on this site from 1088 until 1539, but at the Dissolution it was demolished and the present buildings erected from 1553. Inside are old stocks, a jail, and some of the Saxon coins that were minted in Totnes.

If you plan to visit between May and mid-September, try to make Tuesday the day. Then you will have the chance to visit the market place where locals operate a fully costumed Elizabethan Market; colourful and exciting.

All this history and more can be found by following the Heritage Tour. A 20p booklet from the TIC guides you round the short walk.

Walk straight down High Street, over the river bridge. On reaching the main road turn right and, after a few yards, take the left turn marked Bourton Road. This runs directly into Bourton Lane which plunges downhill and up the far side of the valley. It also changes from paved road to narrow country lane along the way.

Towards the top of this hill is a small well on the left, covered by a stone canopy. Almost opposite, a lane leads off to the right. This is the walk. Follow this green lane until you reach the next – surfaced – road and turn right. 600 yards along on the right is a Public Footpath sign. Pass through the gate. Directly in front is a large slate-roofed house and some barns a little to the left. Aim for the barns, and as you top the brow of a hill, the exit gate will be revealed.

Across is another gate. Pass through it and continue to aim for the barns. On the right of these is a pair of gates. The left hand one carries a footpath arrow pointing right, towards the smaller gate, but this leads into a private orchard. Pass through the larger gate, past the farm and into the road beyond. Turn right and left after 20 yards. Turn left up the steps leading to the church.

The village of Berry Pomeroy is inextricably linked with the Norman family of de la Pomerai. They owned the estate from 1066 until the mid-16th century when it was bought by the Seymour family. The walk follows a path almost round the perimeter of this village, but does see the main attractions. The village church of St. Mary is mainly late 15th century when it was rebuilt by Sir Richard Pomeroy. Other work has been carried out over the years, but it is still a very attractive building with lots of tombs and beautiful fittings. Outside is a sundial dated 1637. Next door is the Manor House with a medieval tithe barn alongside.

Pass the right hand side of the church and out through a lych gate, bearing left. At a road junction, turn left, past the tithe barn and after 100 yards, turn right along a public footpath. After only a few yards, take the left hand of two gates and climb the hill, keeping to the left hand boundary wall. This reaches two more gates. Take the left hand one, cross the road and follow a narrow lane signposted to Berry Pomeroy Castle which leads away to the left.

Around a bend the walk reaches some housing with a lane to the left. This is the entrance to the castle grounds. Follow the lane down through pretty woodland to the castle itself.

Berry Pomeroy castle is believed to have been built in the early 1300s. It remained the family home, passing to the Seymours when they moved into the area. It was damaged during the civil war – the family being strong Royalist supporters – and abandoned when Sir Edward Seymour went to live in Wiltshire at the end of the 17th century.

The ruins are now in the care of English Heritage, and are a 'must'. But beware, Berry Pomeroy Castle is reputed to be the most haunted place in England with not less than nine ghosts.

Follow the road along the front of the castle, and where it starts to go off to the right and a car park, take a downhill track to the left. This continues its way though a bosky hillside before reaching a kissing gate which accesses a road, Keep straight on to a road junction; turn left alongside the little stream and, 100 yards along, take the Public Bridleway to the right. Follow this lane, and as it takes a quite sharp left hand bend approaching some houses, the Bridleway leaves to the right up a track, leaving the paved surface. Down into a valley, over a stream and up the other side, the track reaches woodland. Ignore the path to the right just before the tree line and stay with the bridleway. This bears to the right and eventually reaches a country lane. Cross and continue along the Bridleway.

This reaches a multi-way junction. Take the right hand one onto a semi-paved surface and heading downhill. Ignore the right turn after a few yards and walk to the next T-junction. Turn left here and head towards Marldon.

On the outskirts of this village, a private track leads off right to houses including Channel View. Opposite, on the left, is a minute track with a broken surface leading downhill. Take this and soon the walk reaches the church of St. John the Baptist.

A very ancient church, the tower dating back to 1400, it was built by the Gilbert family who owned Compton castle, a mile to the north. One of the family was the noted explorer Sir Humphrey Gilbert. There are numerous memorials to successive generations of the family inside the church. The Church House Inn serves an excellent pint and carries an old AA circular road sign on the outside wall.

Turn left at the church, right at the next road – by the pub – and first left alongside Jubilee Field, the village's memorial to Queen Elizabeth II's Silver Jubilee. At the next crossroads, walk straight across.

Here is a graphic example of how little treatment was given to Devonian back lanes when they were made up. The surface is broken, revealing the flimsiest skim of tarmac over a stone base; the sort of surface that has existed for centuries. It also shows how close to still being a green lane this – and many others like it – is.

At the end of this lane is a busy dual carriageway. Turn left – not along the old section of road – and some 100 yards along is a break in the Armco barrier. Cross the road here and a Public Footpath leads away from the road. Stay close to the left hand edge and after 150 yards, a stone stile gives access to the next field. Head across the field with the stile to your back, over the brow of a hill towards Stanton Barton farm. A gate gives access to the farmyard. Turn left and immediately right into a narrow lane leading away from these buildings. This soon turns sharp left, with a gate directly ahead and a Public Footpath sign. This leads straight ahead, up mountain and down dale through several gates and stiles for almost a mile.

By now the walk is in a green lane heading downhill. On the

left is a wooden post with a yellow arrow pointing right. Follow this, turn right at the end, and left after 30 yards through an iron gate. This leads to the driveway of Cockington Court; turn left.

Cockington Court was the home of the squires of Cockington from Saxon times. The present building dates back to the 16-17th century, the site having been in the possession of the Cary family from the late 1300s. It was then sold to the Mallocks who owned it until 1927. The local council then acquired it and manage it today. There is a tea room, the gardens are a delight, a mass of yellow daffodils in spring, rhododendrons and azaleas a riot of colour later. A most exquisite cricket field has been fitted into the valley, perhaps the most undulating ground in the country. A player taking up the fielding position of gulley may well be quite literally in one.

At the next fork, keep left, past the thatched gate cottage, to the road, and turn left into Cockington.

This village was designed with picture postcards in mind. Now a tourist honeypot, it is a charming spot with delicately colour-washed thatched cottages, the remains of a blacksmiths, with anvil outside, and a pub and tea room; in fact, all the 'touristy' places to be expected today. Except that this commercialism is kept quite well hidden and does not spoil the essential beauty of the place.

In the far right hand corner of the square is a road with Rose Cottage alongside. Walk up here and take the first right – a No Entry to traffic – into Seaway Lane. At the top of the hill bear right, keeping to Seaway Lane. At Old Mill Road, there is The Manor House Hotel with the road leaving to the left hand side.

Almost at the seafront, on the right is Hennapyn Road. This marks the point where the walk turns left into an unmarked road. A few yards along, the road swings right over the railway bridge, whilst the walk continues alongside the railway and into the station buildings a few yards further.

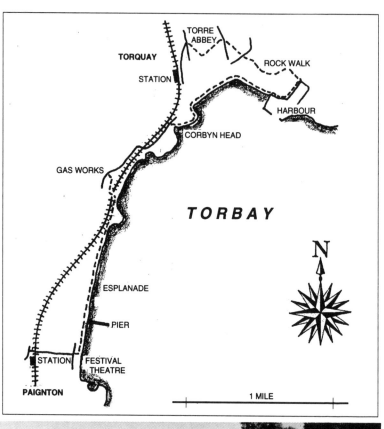

TORQUAY

TORRE ABBEY

ROCK WALK

STATION

HARBOUR

CORBYN HEAD

GAS WORKS

TORBAY

N

ESPLANADE

PIER

STATION

FESTIVAL THEATRE

PAIGNTON

1 MILE

Walk 5
Paignton to Torquay

A short coastal walk alongside some of the most popular holiday beaches in the country. For all that, there are stunning views across Torbay, and, especially out of season, it is possible to combine road and beach walking with a promenade along the prom.

Starting Station: Paignton
Distance: 4 miles
Finishing Station: Torquay
Map: 202
TICs: The Esplanade, Paignton Devon TQ4 6BN – 01803 558383. Vaughan Parade, Torquay, Devon TQ2 5JG – 01803 297428
Problems: Excess crowds at the height of season.

Of Saxon origin, Paignton was some half a mile inland, St. John's Church being at the centre of it. It became a borough with its own weekly market around 1295. Early maps label the place as Paington.

The advent of the railway really started the expansion of the town. Its mild climate saw it in demand for holidays and homes. Several notables have lived around here. Oldway was a 115-room mansion built by the Singer (sewing machine) family in 1874, originally named – incredibly – The Wigwam. Horticulture flourished, and the sweet-tasting Paignton Cabbage was once famed, being despatched to markets all over the country.

Latterly, overtaken by Torquay as *the* resort, Paignton has acquired a slightly tawdry image, more devoted to candy floss and kiss-me-quick hats. Sad, because the place still has much to offer the assiduous seeker of beauty.

Opposite: Part of Torre Abbey, Torquay.

Turn right on leaving the station, and right again, over the level crossing. At the bottom of the road, cross and pass to the left side of the Festival Theatre to the sea front; turn left along The Esplanade.

At the far end of the housing and hotels, Preston Sands finish, and a path leads up alongside the railway. This path runs sharp left over the track and just beyond, on the right, is a gateway leading into Hollicombe Park. Then, head generally left and exit the park opposite the gasworks on the main road.

This half-mile section is not the finest section in this book. It is heavy with traffic, but there really is no alternative. But soon, Corbyn Head hoves into view. It is possible to walk right around this short outcrop, and there are seats on the cliff edge, giving super views over towards Torquay. There are also toilets here.

A path now leads down to both the Promenade and the beach proper, but Torre Abbey Sands can be very busy during the season.

Torquay is a much more recent development; in historical terms. In 1821, less than 2,000 people lived here. Then, the mildness of Torbay winters was publicised, and sufferers from consumption were sent by their doctors. This, allied to the railway's arrival saw a threefold growth in just twenty years, eventually reaching 25,000 by 1871. 'The Queen of Watering Places' had arrived. As with Paignton, the railway helped, although there was a regular steamer service from Portsmouth to Torquay established by 1832. This relieved passengers of the long overland journey from London, substituting a much more tolerable journey down the A3 to Portsmouth.

Early settlers here were families of serving Royal Navy officers. Tor Bay provided an excellent anchorage, sheltered from the prevailing westerly winds, and was well used by ships. The area was such that the whole fleet could comfortably be accommodated. This was particularly true during the Napoleonic Wars of the early 19th century. Then, the fleet spent extended periods at anchor here, officers going ashore at Tor Quay which was originally built by and for the local abbey.

Other hamlets – Ilsham, St. Marychurch, Chelston and Babbacombe were simply swamped in the rush by the gentry to move here and absorbed officially in 1900. Today, over 61,000 people live and enjoy this climate.

Follow the promenade, behind The Princess Theatre and alongside the new marina for as far as you can go before turning left alongside the old harbour. Past the Tourist Information Centre to the road and turn left. Cross by Lloyds Bank and walk along a few yards, crossing the entrance to a multi-storey car park. To the left of this is an alleyway and steps. Climb these and walk along the path which overlooks the harbour from a fair height. This is called Rock Walk, and is cut into the cliff face.

At the far end, turn left, and immediately right into a car park. On the left hand side of this is a narrow passage leading to Belgrave Road. Turn left, and right again at the bowling greens, opposite the Kistor Hotel. At the end of the greens, where the tennis courts start, turn right towards the Riviera Centre, a huge swimming pool and leisure complex. On reaching this building turn left and through a gate to the ruins of Torre Abbey.

This historic building, the oldest in Torbay, was founded in 1196 as a monastery for Premonstratensian Canons, and by the Dissolution was the richest in the land. Much remains of the original building. It was sold for private use, and the present house dates back to the 17th and 18th centuries when the Carey family took over ownership. Ironically, they were Catholics, and converted part of the old guest-hall into a chapel. It remained in that family until purchased by the local corporation in 1930. Subsequently, they have made it into a fascinating museum, as well as being the official residence of the Mayor. The Carey family chapel is retained, and a Memorial Room opened to Torquay's most famous daughter; Dame Agatha Christie, the authoress and creator of Miss Marple and Hercule Poirot. The place is open every day from 1 April to 31 October, and there is a charge for admission.

Pass the front of the Abbey and through the archway, turning right towards the huge greenhouse.

This is a Tropical Plant House with some quite huge specimens, fronds reaching upwards to brush the very high roof. It is the second building on this site, having replaced the original in 1969. There are some very unusual flowering plants, one, a bougainvillaea being a mass of pinky-purple flowers.

Leave the grounds heading towards the far left corner onto Kings Drive. Opposite, at a set of traffic lights, turn left down Falkland Road. This leads into Rathmore Road, and the station is along on the right.

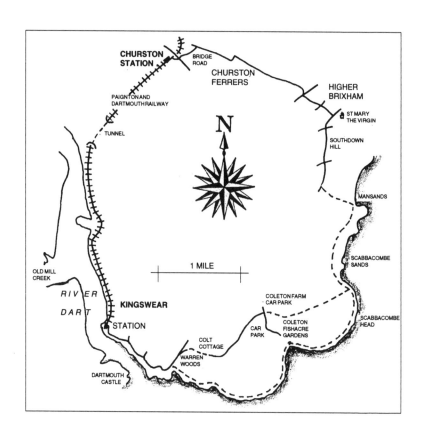

Walk 6
Churston to Kingswear

One of the more strenuous walks in this book, the extra effort is rewarded by stunning views, solitude and a feeling of being at peace with the world. Then, with travel beyond Paignton by steam train, there is a whiff of nostalgia to add to an already heady brew.

Starting Station: Churston/Paignton & Dartmouth Steam Railway
Distance: 8.5 miles or 10 miles following *
Finishing Station: Kingswear – Paignton & Dartmouth Steam Railway
Map: 202
TIC: The Engine House, Mayor's Avenue, Dartmouth, Devon TQ6 9YY; Tel 01803 834224.
Problems: There are three very steep hills to climb, each one up to about 500 feet before plunging down to sea level again. The last hill has a long flight of uneven steps.

Churston station is actually on the edge of Galmpton, now part of the continuous development that is Torbay. There is a pub, The Weary Ploughman, just outside the station,

Leave the station and cross the main road into Bridge Road. Follow this to the end and turn right. A generation ago, it would have been possible to catch a train along this length, as the Brixham branch ran alongside the road to the right. A few earthworks can still be seen. The houses to the left make up Churston Ferrers, its church being the squat tower to the left.

Follow this road towards Brixham, ignoring all the bends until it turns sharp left, leaving a narrow lane, Copythorne Road, on the right. Walk down this to the main road. Directly across is a white cottage that used to be a toll house. Turn left beyond it into Monksbridge Road. This leads to a traffic island and straight on into Horsepool Street and Higher Brixton, the old town, known locally as Cowtown. At the T-junction, a short detour left gives access to the church.

There was a Saxon settlement here as early as the 7th century. It was a fishing village over the years, and late in the last century had nearly 300 boats at sea.

St Mary the Virgin is a gaunt building dating from the early 15th century, and has some interesting carved work inside.

For refreshment, the Waterman's Arms sells Whitbread beer, whilst The Bell proclaims itself to be 'The Inn of St. Mary's'. There are two stores, a Chinese restaurant and takeaway, a bakery and a fruit shop all on hand together with public toilets.

Higher Brixham Church.

Turn right at the junction along Milton Street, past the Blackfriars House, where a monk is reputed to haunt and Higher Brixham Methodist Church, an equally gaunt building. At the next junction take the half left which is Southdown Hill Road, the first of the steep climbs.

A pause as you climb the hill is a good idea; in more ways than one. Look behind you and see the white houses of Torbay stretching away. Ahead, open countryside.

At the brow of the hill, directly ahead, is a post carrying both No Through Road and Bridleway signs. Observe the latter which leads down the hill to Mansands Beach.

The downward path can be tricky underfoot, as it is well used by horses. At the far end of the beach is a ruined building which appears to have been a lime kiln, although there is no documentary evidence to confirm this. There is also a row of cottages where the coastguards used to live. The reason for this remote establishment was believed to have a lot more to do with smuggling than lifesaving.

Walk to the right of the ruin and turn left around the back. A short flight of steps on the right leads to a stile, and into a field behind the cottages. At the gate/stile beyond the cottages is a valley. There are three tracks heading up the other side: take the centre one. There, a stile leads out of that field and continues to climb.

This is a very remote area of National Trust land, known as Woodhuish. There is very little road access and, although occasional visitors make it from the car parks inland, the chances are that you will be undisturbed.

The path stays close to the cliff edge as it levels out briefly before plunging into the next valley and Scabbacombe Sands. A footbridge crosses the stream and the path then leads up a long flight of steps. Before reaching the summit, a signpost points a right hand turn inland to Coleton Farm Car Park. A seat ia available to pause, take breath, and admire the seascape.

The ALTERNATIVE WALK starts here. It is possible to continue along the Coast Path, around Froward Point and rejoin the walk

45

at*. This adds around a mile and a half to the distance, and another drop into a valley and up again.

The inland path continues for almost a mile. On reaching a gate, there is a stile to the right which leads into the car park. Exit this at the far end into the road, walking straight ahead, rather than taking the right hand road. A gate on the left leads to Coleton Fishacre Gardens.

This garden is in the care of the National Trust. It covers some 20 acres, and was created by Dorothy D'Oyly Carte between 1925 and 1940. It is noted for a wide range of rare trees and shrubs, and is open on Wednesday, Thursday, Friday and Sunday from 30 March to 30 September between 10.30am to 5.30pm. Additionally, there is a Sunday opening during March from 2pm to 5pm. The house is not open normally, but arrangements can be made to visit. This must be done by letter in advance.

Carry straight on past another car park. The road then diminishes into a track and passes farm buildings before ending in a turning circle beside Colt Cottage. Ahead, a rocky path continues the walk down into a valley.

A narrow lane is joined by some housing which leads uphill – but not too steeply this time – to a junction where the walk turns left to rejoin the Coast path.

Warren Woods here on the left are dedicated to the memory of Lieutenant Colonel Herbert Jones VC OBE, who was killed during the Falklands conflict. It was opened in June 1984.

* The road now turn towards the north and follows the Dart estuary – still high above the water.

There are some glorious houses along this section, each with a superb view over the water to the Dartmouth side of the river. The whole area is wooded and supremely beautiful.

When the road finally forks, take the left hand one which has a wooden post alongside carrying a yellow arrow and the acorn waymarking symbol. A few yards later, take another left hand fork. This is Beacon Road, which leads to a junction. Bear to the left of the parish church, St. Thomas of Canterbury, down the hill, and the railway station is on the left.

Kingswear is a small town directly opposite Dartmouth. It has little to commend it, save a rather splendid harbour. This is full of yachts of every conceivable shape and size. There are fishing boats unloading their catches – mainly shellfish – on the quay, and a couple of busy ferries crossing to Dartmouth. It was here that General de Gaulle and the Free French were based during the Second World War.

One curiosity can be seen across the water. In the days when the Great Western Railway operated to Kingswear, a ferry linked with the train. So that their passengers would disembark in Dartmouth in GWR style, the company built a station there, but never a railway: what a Trivial Pursuit question!

With a little time to spare, Dartmouth is well worth a visit. It's a lovely town, most of it unspoilt by progress. The Naval College dominates the skyline, a very attractive building. There are castles and quaint streets. Don't miss the elegant Butterwalk, built in 1630, or the Royal Avenue Gardens. There you will find a bandstand, and a memorial to Thomas Newcomen. Living and working in Darmouth, Newcomen created the first practical use of steam power. In 1719 he built a pump large enough to draw water from collieries, allowing coal to be mined below the water table for the first time. There is a recreation of his work, but not locally. A visit to the Black Country Museum at Dudley in the West Midlands is needed for that pleasure.

The steam railway line is a treasure. It runs alongside the river for quite a way before climbing steeply, tunnelling and arriving at the water on the other side of the peninsula. The service operates from Easter to October, and for a few weekends before Christmas.

The Paignton and Dartmouth Steam Railway, Torbay Road, Paignton, Devon TQ4 6AF; Tel 01803 555872. An outline of the history of this railway will be found on Walk 3.

Close to where the railway tunnels, Dame Agatha Christie, doyenne of thriller writers lived until her death. There is much memorabilia associated with her in Torquay museum – see Walk 5, and her house is open to visitors occasionally. Full details from the TIC.

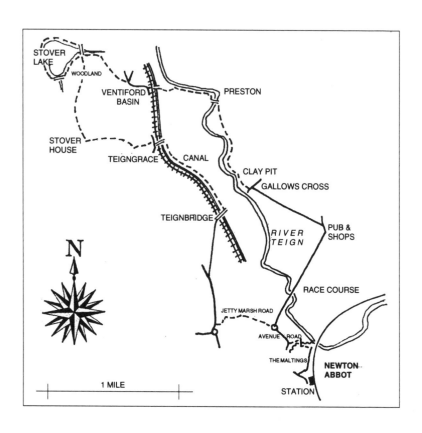

STOVER
LAKE
WOODLAND
VENTIFORD
BASIN
PRESTON
STOVER
HOUSE
TEIGNGRACE
CANAL
CLAY PIT
GALLOWS CROSS
TEIGNBRIDGE
*RIVER
TEIGN*
PUB &
SHOPS
N
RACE COURSE
JETTY MARSH ROAD
AVENUE ROAD
THE MALTINGS
NEWTON
ABBOT
1 MILE
STATION

Walk 7
Newton Abbot Circular

After the physical exertion associated with the last walk, something a little gentler now, as we look at the valley of the river Teign and an old canal. Because of its close proximity to water, this can be a muddy walk when the weather has been less than clement.

Starting Station: Newton Abbot
Distance: 8 miles
Finishing Station: Newton Abbot
Map: 202 and 191
TIC: 6, Bridge House, Courtenay Street, Newton Abbot Devon TQ12 4QS; Tel 01626 67494
Problems: In wet weather – see above. There are also two sections of road walking, one of which is quite busy and, for a short length, has no footpath.

Newton Abbot is very much a recent centre of population. In the 1851 census, there were just 4,000 souls. This had grown to 18,000 at the 1961 count, and almost 21,000 by 1981. It was the arrival of the South Devon railway in 1846 that created the explosion of development; numbers had trebled by the end of that century. The old buildings to the east of the station – opposite the entrance – were used by the railway as a locomotive depot and repair facility. Now they stand empty and forlorn.

A little further along is the building housing the company that probably made the town's name known to a wider audience than any other; David and Charles, the book publishers. Started over 30 years ago by David St. John Thomas, a journalist and author of railway related books, and Charles Hadfield, the greatly respected canal historian, the company achieved eminence in the field of transport titles. Charles sold his interest early in the company's history, but Mr. Thomas developed the business into a multi-million pound enterprise before selling to Readers Digest in the late 1980s.

The first record of settlement in the area was in 1196 when Shireborne Newton was noted. There are few buildings of any antiquity in Newton Abbot, even the churches are new. The only real item is St. Leonard's Tower, which is all that remains of a 14th century church demolished in 1836.

Leave the station and head towards the right into Queens Street. Take the first on the right which is Quay Road, and turn left into Teign Road.

Tuckers Mill, on the right, is looked at towards the end of Walk 8.

At the end, turn left alongside the river, and after a few yards, use the footbridge to gain access to the right bank. This leads into Wharf Road, and at the end, turn right into Avenue Road, right again at the traffic island and follow the road past the race-course and Tesco. Carry on to the T-junction; turn left.

On this junction is refreshment in several guises. The Smugglers fish and chip shop is opposite, with the Kings Arms next door. This sells Heavitree Ales. On the corner is a typical small shop that offers a variety of snacks and drinks.

After about 50 yards, Broadway Road bears off to the left, with a Natwest bank on the corner. Take this turn and follow it to the far end at Gallows Cross.

In the distance, straight ahead, the forbidding hills of Dartmoor can be seen. Haytor, the rocky outcrop over a thousand feet above sea level, is prominent.

Ahead, but slightly to the left, is a gate and Public Footpath sign. This is the walk. It follows the edge of a huge claypit, high above the river, before plunging downhill to water level. Follow this path for almost a mile. It leads briefly away from the river bank before returning as it meets a wider path. Resist the temptation to turn left here: it leads nowhere. A short distance along, at Preston, there is a left turn that passes down steps to a bridge over the Teign. At the far side turn right, picking up The Templar Way, a description of which can be found in Walk 8.

Before long, the path bears left, away from the main river, following a small tributary. Pass through a gate and under a railway bridge at Ventiford Basin before turning right.

The railway was originally a branch line to Mortonhampstead, opened in 1866. Then, in 1882, a further branch was built north towards Ashton, and extended through the delightfully named Doddiscombleigh into Exeter in 1903. The remnants of this line can be seen, south of Exeter St. Thomas' station on the right heading south. Passenger services were withdrawn in 1958, those from the Mortonhampstead line on 2 May 1959. All that remains today is a single track to the English China Clay workings near Heathfield. They ship out vast quantities of ball clay by road to Teignmouth for export (see Walk 8), and a train-load most days.

Keep to the left at Teigngrace Cross, the next junction – ignoring the Templer Way signs. Follow this lane until a road joins from the right, and a few yards along is a Templer Way sign to the left. Take this path into the woodland. On reaching the water, turn left and follow this to Stover Lake. The walk turns left, but a bridge over the water on the right gives a good view of the lake. It is possible to add almost another mile to the walk here by circumnavigating the lake. If you take this option, turn right over the bridge, and follow the water. You eventually return to the same point.

Covering some 11 acres, the lake is a Site of Special Scientific Interest. Duck frequently 'in residence' include teal, pochard, tufted duck, shoveller, goldeneye and mallard. Coots, herons, canada geese, snipe and water rail are also to be seen. Depending on the season, the hedgerows hold tits, nuthatch and goldcrest. Crossbills, siskin, chaffinch and even a firecrest are also regular visitors.

After only a few yards, the path splits; take the left-hand fork with the Templer Way waymark. Over a bridge, and Stover House, formerly the home of the Templer family, can be seen to the right. At the end of this path, bear left into what was a driveway to the house.

Down a gentle slope, there is a clay store on the right. The Templer Way leaves to the left.

Cross this field and pass through a pretty iron gateway to the road and turn right. As this road turns right after reaching some housing, a lane to the left is marked Private Road to Teign Manor and The Barns. Cleverly camouflaged on the wall is The Templer Way sign. Cross the railway – taking care to look out for approaching trains, and at the derelict canal lock, turn right.

This settlement is Teigngrace, essentially a creation of the Templers. The church, St. Peter and St. Paul, was funded by them, and rebuilt in 1872.

James Templer, landowner, was responsible for exploiting the ball clay found in the Teign basin. This is a highly prized commodity for pottery manufacturers, producing a fine finish, and being almost white after its first (biscuit) firing. To transport this clay, he decided on water, and The Stover or Teigngrace Canal was built in 1790. It ran from the River Teign near Newton Abbot to Ventiford. It seems that there were once plans to build as far as Bovey Tracey, but they were never executed.

The two mile long line opened in 1794, and was soon very busy with trade. There were five locks to be constructed including a staircase pair. This method of construction is effectively two chambers joined together without an intervening length of water and uses the bottom gate of one as the top gate of the other. Thus, a sharp fall can be achieved in a short distance. The Stover Canal locks were of a most unusual size: 110 feet x 14 feet: barges were constructed 54 feet long, and two could fit in the chamber at once. Loading alongside the canal, barges would lock down into the Teign and sail down to Teignmouth where the clay would be trans–shipped into coasters for the hazardous journey around Land's End into the River Mersey and Liverpool.

Traffic along the canal continued to increase over the years. Then, George Templer – James' son – opened a granite quarry at Haytor on the eastern edge of Dartmoor and around seven miles away from Ventiford. For transport, he built a tramway down to the canal which opened in 1820. The volume of trade was such that a new quay at Teignmouth was soon needed. George Templer again built this, but its date of first use is a matter of dispute between historians: 1825 and 1827 are both used by various learned scholars.

Haytor Granite Railway was unique in that the track was made from granite setts laid lengthways and cut with a flange to hold the wagon wheels in place. It was worked by horses and eventually there were six quarries in production, with some ten miles of track in use. Granite flowed along the canal in great quantity.

The barges originally used sails as their method of propulsion. An unusual arrangement of sails was used, believed to be the last commercial use of a Viking-style rig.

There was a financial hiatus in the Templer household by 1829, forcing George to sell the canal to raise money. The Duke of Somerset took it over, and it continued to trade well for the next thirty years. Then, the Moretonhampstead and South Devon Railway appeared on the scene. They needed land in the area, and ended up not only with the land, but the canal as well. The clay trade was still thriving, but the tramway from Haytor had fallen into disuse by 1858.

Once the railway became owners, the canal was leased out to a local company, and shortened by the closure of the northernmost half mile. The

Great Western Railway eventually took over ownership and, although they purposely neglected other canals they inherited, forcing trade onto rail, the Stover was allowed to continue trading. The final recorded traffic was in 1939, and the canal abandoned in 1942.

The lock chamber, still in fair condition, is the fifth and final one on the canal.

At the railway crossing, a little wry humour – probably unintentional – can be seen. To illustrate the potential danger, an InterCity 125 express train is depicted: on a freight-only line with a speed limit of 20mph.

Walk alongside the canal to the next road bridge at Teignbridge Crossing. Here, leave the canal, turn right and follow the road to the main road, bear left and walk towards Newton Abbot. Over the brow of a hill and down into the dip, the road starts to rise again towards a traffic island. Here, there is an unmarked left hand turn. This is Jetty Marsh Road, take this, and at the next parting of the ways at a right hand bend, take the right hand track. This leads back to Avenue Road at the traffic island encountered on the outward leg. Use the reverse route to return to the station.

But if you feel the need for sustenance, take the right turn into Queen Street, just before the station. There, in the space of a couple of hundred yards, you have the choice of a fish and chip shop, three Chinese restaurants and takeaway, a Balti Restaurant, a Cantonese Restaurant, a Kentucky Fried Chicken, a Steak-Away, an Italian and French Restaurant, a Tandoori Restaurant, an Indian Restaurant, Fozzies Food Bar (Sandwiches) and The Park Cafe. The residents of this fair town must be inveterate diners-out.

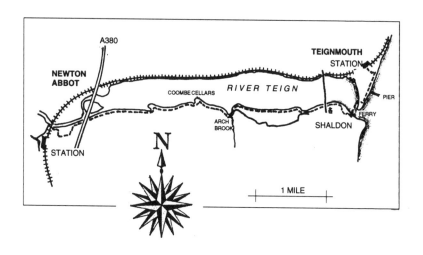

The ferry crossing from Teignmouth to Shaldon.

Walk 8
Teignmouth to Newton Abbot

If you are looking for a walk completely devoid of hills – not easy to find in Devon – then this is the one for you. But, in case you think the county is going to let you down, it can involve a few lengths of undulation. The reason for this is the tide: see below.

Staring Station: Teignmouth
Distance: 6.5 miles
Finishing Station: Newton Abbot
Map: 192 and 202
TICs: The Den, Seafront, Teignmouth, Devon TQ 14 8BE; Tel 01626 779769. 6, Bridge House, Courtenay Street, Newton Abbot, Devon TQ 12 4QS; Tel 01626 67494
Problems: There is a short ferry crossing at Teignmouth which is fairly reliable, but can be suspended due to bad weather. There is a road alternative. Part of the walk alongside the estuary is affected by tides. It is impassable for four hours either side of high water. The TICs have tide tables. When the tide is in, there is another route along the road.

Teignmouth has a lot going for it. To the east of the station is a sandy beach, a pier and the usual seaside attractions. The town centre is a charming amalgam of old and new, with traffic-free areas and a delightful range of pubs.

Its main claim to fame though is nautical. It has a reasonable harbour, which has been used from very early days. The French sacked the place in 1340 and again in 1690, when it was rebuilt by national subscription, and the fishing fleet here was trading with Newfoundland as early as the 18th century. In the harbour today there are always ships of up to 3,000 tons to be found. These are regularly employed carrying ball clay for export, and bringing in animal feedstuffs and fertiliser.

The last major development of the port was in the 1820s. George Templer, anxious to improve his ability to ship out clay, had the work carried out, and subsequently granite from Haytor on Dartmoor also moved through the port. More information about the Templers and their industry is contained in Walk 7.

Oddly, Teignmouth came in for some destruction during the last war. The Luftwaffe carried out regular raids between 1940 and 1943, killing some 3% of the population.

|| Leave the station and cross the car park to the left hand exit. Cross
|| the road and head left towards Teignmouth Museum.

Sadly, this fascinating small museum is a summer only attraction, and thus denied to off-season walkers. It opens over the Easter weekend and then again from May until the end of September.

|| Walk down French Street and at the end turn right. Almost across
|| the road is an alleyway between The Aphrodite Restaurant and
|| The Bookworm. This leads to the sea front. Gain the Promenade
|| and turn right.
|| Past the pier the walk reaches a car park with the lifeboat road
|| beyond. On this slipway is the ferry across the river to Shaldon.

The ferry sails on demand across The Salty from 7.45am to dusk every day from Easter to the end of October. Off season, it is from 8am to 5pm and there are no sailings on Saturday or Sunday, or in really bad weather. The ferryman is delightfully garrulous: quite a character. In the space of a ten minute crossing you will receive a potted history of his life, and probably reveal much of your own. If the ferry is not operating, it is still possible to complete this walk, even if it does mean missing a lump of the fun. Retrace the course of Walk 9 from Teignmouth station to Shaldon Bridge, which crosses the river to Shaldon church. Rejoin the walk at *.

|| On reaching *terra firma* again, turn right past The Ferry Boat Inn
|| and follow the road inland. Take the first right that leads down to
|| the riverside, and follow this until it returns to the main road; turn
|| right. Bear right at the library, past The London Inn and alongside
|| the church to Bridge Road.

This bridge across the Teign replaced the original 1827 structure that was the longest in the country. This has an opening section to allow shipping through.

Once there were three shipbuilders in Ringmore, but the trade died after dredging in the river ceased.

The Parish Church of St. Peter The Apostle is a very unusual building. One of Sir John Betjeman's favourites, its squat bulky appearance is due to its relative youth, and the fact that it is built on unstable ground. It was consecrated on 29 July 1903, having taken some eight years to build. The barrel-vaulted roof made from stone slabs is unusual – and heavy, going some way to explaining the somewhat ugly buttressing on the exterior. No tower was built, again because of the ground.

Inside is fascinating. Marble abounds, particularly on the pulpit. The base is black, eight pinkish pillars support the grey pulpit pedestal and a flight of carpeted polished steps give access. Beautifully carved stone columns around the edge are infilled with greenish marble: exquisite.

And the font: is it unique? A white marble statue of St. John The Baptist holds a giant clamshell which carries the water. Again, breathtaking.

There is very little stained glass, but a huge west window of clear glass provides lots of natural light. The organ, rebuilt about ten years ago, has three manuals, and is reckoned by those who know about these things to produce one of the finest tones in Devon. Judging from the type of services held, and the fact that confessions are taken, it can only be described as 'high church'.

If ever there was a case for 'not judging the book by its cover', this is surely it.

   * Cross the road and take the path alongside the river signposted The Templer Way.

At the entrance to this track can be seen an old milepost. It indicates the distances to Torquay, Brixham, Dartmo (Dartmouth) and Totnes in miles, furlongs and poles.

The Templer Way is a 15 mile walk from Shaldon to Haytor quarry high in the Dartmoor hills. The route gets its name from the Templer family. Up in the hills, a tramway was built to move the granite, some of which was used in the construction of London Bridge, The British Museum and The National Gallery, to the Stover Canal (Details in Walk 7), and then downriver to Teignmouth.

Some 200 yards along a Templer Way Information Board fills in a little of the background to this area. Beyond, at the road turn right and walk along this lane past the castellated Ringmore Towers which is nothing more than holiday apartments.

On reaching The Strand, a right turn to the shore and then left, or straight on up the road: it's decision time.

You will need an hour to walk from here to Arch Brook. This is the section affected by the tide. Do *not* attempt it if you are within four hours of high tide. There are a couple of headlands to walk round and you will be cut off with no recognised escape route. If in doubt, follow the road.

Whichever route you take, the walk arrives at an inlet where a stream enters the Teign. If you are on the shore, this is best crossed by using the road bridge, rejoining the estuary on the other side. The path continues along the waterside to Coombe Cellars.

Coombe Cellars Inn.

This is a rather splendid restaurant and pub with an unrivalled view across the river. Sundays is a great time here, with a water-ski jump close by and much other water-based sports activity.

Bear left through the car park, regaining the walk alongside the sea wall. This follows a causeway that bridges another stream, keeping to the right; ignore the stile to the left.

Stay with the river and The Templer Way under a new road bridge until the path leaves the river, crosses another tributary and becomes a road through an industrial estate. This eventually turns sharp left, but a track leads right to Town Quay. On reaching the river, turn left, pass under the railway and take the first road on the left, away from the river. This is Teign Road.

The massive stone building on the left is Tuckers Maltings. Although open in summer as a tourist attraction, the only one in the country, it is actually a working maltings, producing enough malt to make 15 million pints of beer every year. It covers 75,000 square feet and offers lots of 'hands on' experiences. This is a splendid place to learn about this process and how it has evolved over the years. In the 19th century there were thousands of these places: now there are only seven.

|| At the end of Teign Road, a right turn into Quay Road. At the top, turn left and the station is a few yards along on the left.

A description of Newton Abbot is to be found in Walk 7.

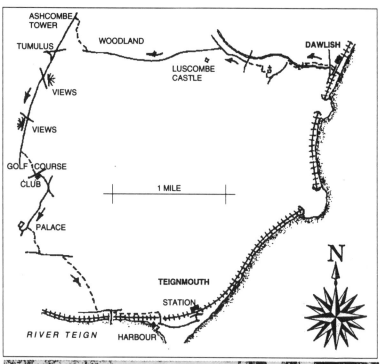

ASHCOMBE
TOWER

WOODLAND

TUMULUS

LUSCOMBE
CASTLE

DAWLISH

VIEWS

VIEWS

GOLF COURSE

CLUB

1 MILE

PALACE

N

TEIGNMOUTH

STATION

RIVER TEIGN

HARBOUR

Dawlish.

Walk 9
Dawlish to Teignmouth

This is predominantly a scenic walk. The sea views are some of the best and highest to be found on these walks, but the drawback is that much of it involves roads rather than paths. However, most are quiet and the occasional intrusion of the 'infernal confusion' engine does not detract too much.

Starting Station: Dawlish
Distance: 8.5 miles
Finishing Station: Teignmouth
Map: 192
TICs: The Lawn, Dawlish, Devon EX7 9PW; Tel 01626 863589.
The Den, Sea Front, Teignmouth, Devon TQ14 8BE; Tel 01626 779769
Problems: One long uphill section

Leave the station, turning left and walk down to the main road. Turn right and walk alongside the shops to a pedestrian crossing. This leads, half left, across both sections of a dual carriageway and straight into a park. Pick up the side of the river – Dawlish Water – and follow it through the recreation area known as The Lawn.

It was around 1790 that Dawlish began to attract visitors. Named after the stream which had the Saxon appellation *Doflisc* – Black Water back in 1044, it grew in popularity after the arrival of the railway in 1846. With a resident population of over 10,000, expanding hugely in summer, the town has produced a splendid amalgam of architectural styles.

The original town was much further back from the sea, centred around the parish church of St. Gregory the Great. The exterior of that building shows dramatically its history of rebuilding. The red sandstone tower is 14th century, the rest is 19th, but in two disparate styles. There are shops of every kind here

61

and all the variety of refreshment one could need.

One charming aspect of the riverside walk is the number and variety of water birds living there. Hundreds of mallards, waterhens and seagulls are augmented, according to the season by swans and a fascinating selection of wild duck. Even the handsome male mandarin duck visits occasionally.

At the end of the bowling green, a bridge takes the walk across the water to the left hand bank. Continue up here for as far as you can go. Even at the end of Brunswick Place, the path continues along, to the right hand side of a toilet block.

On its passage through Dawlish, the river is delicately landscaped, with the banks slightly built up, but the work is never overpowering. There are small waterfalls every few yards, each with a slope at one side to allow ducks and other wildlife to access the next pool. Palm trees grow in profusion along the banks, and the whole creates an attractive centrepiece for the town.

When the path eventually runs out, just below some housing, turn left and walk up to Barton Road; turn right. At the end, a left turn takes you in the direction of the police station alongside the churchyard wall on the right. At the end of this is a gateway back into the yard. Take it, pass to the left of the church building, through another gate and turn left.

On reaching the road, take the one directly ahead, but pause to admire an attractive overbridge just to the left that is part of the entrance driveway to Luscombe Castle.

Luscombe Castle was built between 1800 and 1804 by the famed architect John Nash. The owner was Charles Hoare, the banker. He employed Humphrey Repton to lay out the gardens. It is a fine building, even today, and the now mature grounds are exquisite. Regrettably, the whole area is in private hands, with no public access allowed. As the walk progresses, there are several good views of both the house and grounds.

Now begins the long climb. Follow the road around the perimeter of the Castle grounds, passing a couple of entrances guarded by gatehouses. After a mile and a half, there is a Public Footpath pointing into the woods to the right. This continues to climb slightly through the woodland, eventually arriving at a road: turn left. As you do so, admire the creatures guarding the entrance to the house opposite: two stone wild boars.

At the next crossroads carry straight on, and at the next, bear left. The views are constant here, a deep grassy valley and the sea beyond. On reaching the next (rather busy) road, cross straight over and at the following junction, make a small detour left.

The road runs straight across Teignmouth Golf Club. This course was designed by Alistair MacKenzie, who was also responsible for that most elegant and challenging of courses at Augusta, Georgia – home of the US Masters tournament. One tee, alongside the road, is named Siberia, a reflection on the almost ceaseless wind that blows up there. The views are majestic. The east Devon coast around Exmouth and beyond is plain to see. The cliff tops there are visited on Walk 12.

Having admired the views, return to the junction, turn left along-side the golf course. Over to the right, the eastern edge of Dartmoor can be seen. After a few yards, a Public Footpath leads off to the left across the links: beware of flying golf balls. After several turns, all well signposted, the path reaches a road, turn left, and right at the entrance to the golf club.

Down the hill, there is a right turn signposted Bishopsteign-ton. This is a steeply downhill section. As the gradient eases, there is a Public Footpath sign to the left, but ignore that for a few moments and walk to the farm entrance a few yards along on the right.

There it is possible to see the remains of The Bishop's Palace. This was one of the country residences of the medieval Bishops of Exeter. It was built by John Grandisson, bishop from 1327 to 1369 on land owned by the church from before the Norman conquest. By 1501 it was derelict; now it is scheduled as an Ancient Monument. Although on private land, visits can be arranged. A plaque outside the gates gives full details of the site and its current owners.

Return to the footpath, and down the lane which leads to a farm. At a metal gate, there is a small wooden one to the right with a Footpath sign pointing through. This leads to a lane where the walk turns left. Some 600 yards along here, another Public Footpath sign leads through a gate to the right and down the valley towards the sea. A mile along here, this terminates quite abruptly at a main road. Turn left, taking extreme care on this busy road with no footpath for some 200 yards.

At the first traffic lights, cross and follow the road down to

Shaldon bridge. On the left, just before the railway is a path that leads around the edge of a water pumping station, right to the railway, and left through a gate.

Keep close to the railway, up an embankment close to some new houses and into Bitton Park with the attractive Georgian Bitton House on the hill. Walk through the park and take the right hand path at the end of the trees which leads back to the railway. At the bottom of here, turn left into Alexandra Terrace. At the far end it is possible to see the small port of Teignmouth which is usually active with ships being loaded. There is a flight of steps leading to an alleyway just to the right of the Job Centre. This in turn leads to a footbridge over the railway on the right.

Take this, follow the road round to the left and the right until you arrive almost opposite the vehicle entrance to the harbour: turn left. After only a few yards, turn right at The Blue Anchor pub which, unusually for this area, sells Boddington's Manchester Ales. This is Teign Street which in turn leads into Bank Street and then Wellington Street.

On the left is Lloyds Bank. Here, a left turn into Station Road. At the end, turn right, and a few yards along is a path through the hedge which gives access to the main road and, across, the station.

A detailed look at Teignmouth can be found at the beginning of Walk 8.

Walk 10
Exeter Central to Exeter St. Thomas

Plymouth (See Walk Two) and Exeter are the only cities in Devon. The latter was a Roman settlement, has a mass of history, fascinating streets, and is well worth exploration. It also proves – if it were necessary – that city walks, whilst perhaps not as invigorating as country ones, pack in a wealth of interest to compensate.

Starting Station: Exeter Central
Distance: 3.5 or 4.5 miles
Finishing Station: Exeter St. Thomas or St David's
Map: 192
TIC: Civic Centre, Paris Street, Exeter, Devon EX1 1JJ; Tel 01392 265700
Problems: Infrequent train service to St. Thomas. St. David's is a pleasant extra mile along the river bank.

Again, because of the sheer volume of history and current fascination, our look at Exeter must be somewhat superficial. And, as with so much English history, the city's record is one of almost continual turbulence.

There was a Celtic settlement before the Romans arrived to establish the city in 50 AD. During their tenure the place prospered, and a Wall was built, much of which remains today. After their departure, it was the site of intermittent skirmishes particularly in 876 and 893 when the Danes laid seige. They were back again in 1003, this time sacking the city. Edward the Confessor was king at the time, and, with a monastery, the town was rebuilt. He also established the Diocese in about 1050, enthroning Leofric as the first Bishop.

The town resisted the Norman conquest for two years, and after it fell,

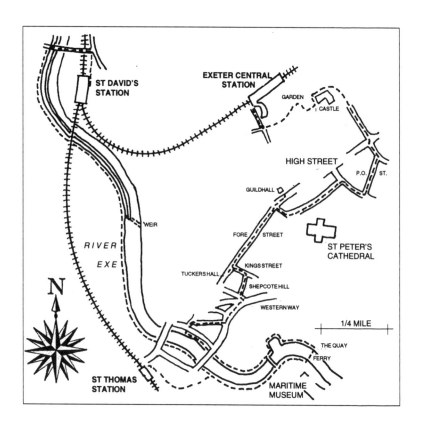

the Normans built Rougemont Castle. Next to disturb the peace was the Flemish pretender to the throne, Perkin Warbeck. He landed in Cornwall in 1497 and, gathering an army of six thousand around him, attacked Exeter, but failed to conquer. He did get inside the gates shortly afterwards: in chains, as Henry VII had him dragged off to the Tower of London where he was eventually executed.

Henry VIII granted the town its Charter in 1537. It became The County and City of Exeter, and was then entitled to hold its own assizes and appoint a sheriff.

When the Reformation came, there was a rebellion centred on the Exeter area, who wanted to retain the Roman church. Considering that Devon became a centre of non-conformism, this was strange. Eventually a battle was fought between the two sides, which saw a crushing defeat of the rebels. Over four thousand Devonians died, either in battle or by execution afterwards. A more detailed account of this insurrection can be found in Walk 14.

Next upheaval was the Civil War. After a brief occupation by Parliamentarians, it was taken over by Cavaliers and held until Charles fled in 1646, when the city was handed to General Fairfax.

It was during the reign of James II that the Duke of Monmouth rebelled and was defeated at the Battle of Sedgemoor in 1685. The Duke of Beaufort's Musketeers – later to become The Devonshire Regiment – were raised to defend the king here. This event led to Judge George Jeffries holding one of his infamous Bloody Asssize's at Exeter when eighty rebels were hanged.

By far the most destructive event in recent years was the bombing of Exeter in May 1942. There were no real military reasons for these attacks; just acts of wanton destruction. Much of the centre was razed, and over 400 shops and 36 pubs and clubs destroyed.

Leave Central Station and turn left, taking the first left up Northernhay into Northernhay Gardens. This area of peace has a fine selection of statues to various worthies from over the centuries. Halfway up the slope, turn right, through a low archway towards Rougemont Castle and Gardens. Take the left hand path which climbs steeply to a wall, pass through the archway and follow the path back down.

On leaving the Gardens, walk down Northernhay Place and cross the road using the arcade to gain High Street.

On the left in an intiguing attraction. The Underground Passages is a guided tour of some 35 minutes which looks at the two water systems built by the city and the cathedral. They are over 500 years old, and run through the remains of one of the old city gates. Details from 01392 265887.

|| Turn right and first left at Maples store. Around this corner is the Phoenix Fountain, erected there in 1992, the 50th anniversary of the Blitz, in memory of those who lost their lives.

Turn right into Post Office Street where the Roman wall is clearly in evidence, and right at the end into Bedford Street. This was the central area for bomb damage.

On the corner, by the new Post Office, is a plaque that notes the existence of a Dominican Convent on the site from 1259 to 1539. It also notes the birth here in 1544 of Princess Henrietta, daughter of Charles I.

|| Towards the end, by Goldsmith Ltd., turn left into Catherine Street. On the left are the ruins of Annuellars House.

On this site, recently excavated, have been found the remains of a Roman fortress, dated between 55 and 60 AD. The Annuellars house was built on the site afterwards, that lasting until 1858. The chantry priests lived here. It was then converted into four separate houses, one of which became The Country House Inn. This was bombed. A few yards along, another of the city's more impressive buildings is the Oddfellows Hall.

|| The lane then leads into Cathedral Yard. Keep to the right, taking the right turn, Broadgate, back into High Street; turn right.

Both inside and out, the Cathedral is one of England's architectural glories. The building as we know it today was started in 1275. As with most buildings of its type, it suffered during the Reformation, and again during the war. But restoration has produced the wonder we see today. From outside, the dramatic flying buttresses are compelling to the eye. But inside, breathtaking is the only word to describe. Look down the nave. Over 300 feet of Gothic vaulting, the longest in the world. The graceful sweeping lines, the elaborate carvings: craftsmanship supreme. And one – wholly unexpected – benefit from the attentions of the Luftwaffe was that the amount of repair work needed then has ensured that the building today is in far better condition than many of its contemporaries.

In Broadgate, it is possible to see the location of the old city gate, There were seven of these, originally licensed in 1286. This one was removed in 1825.

|| Walk a few yards up High Street to The Guildhall.

This is the oldest functioning municipal building in the country. Built in 1330, it was improved in 1468, whilst the portico was added during the reign of Elizabeth I in about 1594. The Turks Head pub, next door, is a delightfully quaint and tiny building.

|| Turn around, walk back along High Street and down Fore Street.

On the left, the church of St. Petrock is no longer consecrated, being currently under conversion to a day centre for the homeless. St. Olaves, a little further on the right is still used as a place of worship. Further down the hill on the right, Tuckers Hall is another interesting medieval work, dating from 1471. Exeter became the regional capital for wool and its associated trades; The Worshipful Company of Weavers, Fullers and Shearmen of the City of Exeter ruled the roost in these parts for many a long year. Tuckers were makers of the ornamental frills that covered the neck and shoulders of ladies dresses.

|| Turn around and walk back up Fore Street for a few yards until reaching King Street on the right. Take that turn and the first right again. This is Stepcote Hill.

A delightful cobbled street of medieval appearance, with stepped walkway and a central run-off for rain water: plus whatever else was tipped into the streets in previous centuries! At the bottom is The House that Moved.

Originally located in Edmund Street, close by, it was in the way of a new road scheme in 1961. Rather than demolish such a treasure, the whole structure was moved on rollers to its present site, close to West Gate. This corner is a delight, with a couple of very old shops, and St. Mary's Church adding a little dignity to an otherwise rather frivolous scene.

|| Walk towards the new road and cross the first carriageway before turning right. This leads over what was once an Exe bridge with gatehouse. Turn left, and at the end enter the subway turning right up the slope. This brings the walk to the current course of the River Exe. Turn left along the bank. Pass under the steel footbridge and into the area of the old port.

The buildings in this area are some of the best preserved in the country. A television series – 'The Onedin Line' – was shot here because it offered the most authentic locations the producers could find. The first brick house in Exeter was built in 1681 as Customs House, now an Ancient Monument, and still used by Customs and Excise. There are shops, a museum and toilets.

'The House that Moved', Western Way, Exeter.

The next move is dependent on circumstances. At the quay, a ferry crosses to the far bank. It runs most of the summer, and some of the winter. At 10p it's a fun way to arrive across the other side. Failing that, walk back to the iron bridge, cross and walk down the other side to the Exeter Maritime Museum.

This wonderful collection of boats was the brainchild of Major David Goddard. Walking round the area in 1963, and struck by the total neglect and impending dereliction, he had already considered the idea of assembling boats from around the world and finding a permanent home for them. Then, with 23 boats, including some Arab craft he had collected on his last posting to Bahrain, the museum opened in June 1969. Traumas were to strike early in this decade, and for a time it looked as though the collection would be dispersed. But today, all appears rosy again.

Before leaving along the canal, the basin area itself is worthy of a brief exploration. At the head of the basin, in the ground, is some railway track and an old wagon turntable. This was part of a short goods railway to City Basin built by the South Devon Railway in 1867. Originally, it used Brunel's broad (7 feet) gauge, but in 1871 a third rail was added to allow standard gauge London and South West Railway traffic to use it.

Walk back alongside the river, keeping to the left hand bank. On reaching Gervaise Avenue, turn left and follow the road round to the right. At the next main road turn left and St. Thomas station is a few yards along.

If you choose to walk back to St. David's, keep to the river bank, past the weir, under the railway and along to the next road bridge. Turn right, cross the railway lines, and a gate just beyond gives access to a car park and the station forecourt beyond.

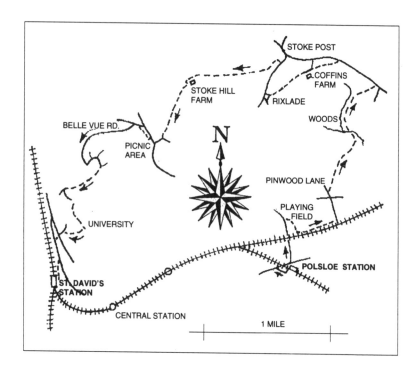

STOKE POST

COFFINS FARM

STOKE HILL FARM

RIXLADE

WOODS

BELLE VUE RD.

PICNIC AREA

N

PINWOOD LANE

UNIVERSITY

PLAYING FIELD

POLSLOE STATION

ST DAVID'S STATION

CENTRAL STATION

1 MILE

Walk 11
Polsloe Bridge to
Exeter St. David's

This walk circles the northern ends of the city of Exeter, and graphically illustrates that it is possible to walk mainly in magnificent countryside whilst always being very close to a city. There are no points of riveting interest along the way; just pleasant, varied scenery. Exeter itself is dealt with in detail on Walk 9.

Starting Station: Polsloe Bridge
Distance: 6 miles
Finishing Station: Exeter St. Davids
Map: 192
TIC: Civic Centre, Paris Street, Exeter EX1 1JJ; Tel 01392 265700
Problems: None

Leave the station down the steps turning right and right again, under the railway. Cross the road and turn left by the Shell garage into Beacon Lane.

There are several facilities here. A pub, The Queens Head, is a free house, with a newsagent selling the basic necessities close by. A fish and chip shop opposite Beacon lane is well located if pre-walk fortification is required.

Walk under the Waterloo - Exeter line bridge, round a bend until you reach Betty's Mead Playing Fields on the right. Through the entrance and head back towards the railway embankment. Bear left and walk alongside this, through a gate into a well used track until you reach the next road. Turn left.

At the top of this road is a crossroads. Head straight across, up Pinwood Lane. After 120 yards, there is a Public Bridleway sign pointing to the right. This is a well used green lane, and the course of the walk. It leads away from housing, across an open area, over the brow of a hill and into a valley. At the next gate, ford the stream and turn left. The path is clearly defined with red markers on trees and fences.

By now, the strollers who frequented the path earlier are left behind, and this exquisite area of woodland is very quiet. The path follows roughly the course of a stream, over a meadow and back into more trees. Here, the path moves uphill, away from the water and through a gate into a field. The course across is dictated by a solitary tree straight ahead. Aim for this, and beyond the top of this hill is a gate into a lane. Turn left.

After half a mile there is the option. A public footpath to the left leads across fields to a track giving access to Goffins Farm. This track leads to another short path which eventually reaches to a paved road at Rixlade. Turn right, up the hill until you reach a Public Bridleway sign pointing left.

Alternatively, stay with the road until you reach a T-junction at Stoke Post, turn left (signposted Exeter) and 250 yards along on the right is the same bridleway.

The views from along this path are spectacular, overlooking a valley with steep hills beyond. Directly below, but hidden by trees is where the river Culm, arriving from the north-west, feeds into the Exe from the north. Both these valleys stretch away into the distance. The pretty village of Stoke Canon is the only real settlement of any size, with the Exeter to Paddington railway skirting it to the north. The earthworks which once carried the Tiverton railway line from Stoke Canon can be clearly seen curving away to follow the Exe.

Follow the Bridleway through the gate into a field and alongside a fence guarding a large white house. At the end of this fence, turn left, and the gate directly ahead gives access to a field. The official exit to this is currently blocked, so head half right to a gate in the far corner. Through this gate, turn left, and ahead is another gate with wooden fence alongside. This is the Bridleway.

After half a mile, this leads into a metalled lane which then leads to a 'main' road. Just before the end of this, a short ramp on the left leads down into another road: ignore it. At the main road, turn right, up the hill. On the brow of the hill is an entrance to the left. Make sure you don't take the one a few yards before the crest of the hill. In this gateway, a track leads to a car park and picnic tables, with another fine view over the Exe valley, this time looking west towards the lowering range of hills known as Dartmoor.

To the right, a fingerpost points towards Wrefords Lane, a path that runs parallel with the road. At the end, a narrow crush leads into a lane: turn left, down the hill. A few yards along on the left is Belle Vue Road. This is marked Private at this end (but not the other). Two residents quizzed along here were quite relaxed about pedestrians using it: it's motor traffic they don't want. If you do fall foul of anyone, there is an alternative. Carry straight on down the hill, take the second on the left which drops you eventually to the main road. Turn left for St. David's station.

Belle Vue Road drops steeply downhill, past a few very attractive houses clinging to the side of a valley. One has a blue winged horse on its roof. The owner was part of the airborne Normandy Landings in 1944. His drop-zone? Pegasus Bridge. In this valley, the locals occasionally see roe deer; more often, foxes and badgers. And this, within the boundaries of the City of Exeter.

Having arrived on a made-up road surface again, pass the porter's lodge of Exeter University and take the left turn up Belvidere Road. After 75 yards, there is a fork in the road; take the right into Clydesdale Road. This turns into a track, and then back into a road. By now the number of students around make you realise that this is the university.

At the first building on the right, take a path downhill to the right marked 'Birks Hall.' At the bottom, bear slightly right to regain a road, and then turn left. This arrives at a main road. Across, slightly to the left is a pathway leading down to another road alongside the railway. Follow this, cross the road and Exeter St. Davids Station is on the right.

There are several refreshment points close to the station. The Red Cow Inn serves the local brew, Heavitree. The Jolly Porter is also close by as is the Great Western Hotel with the Brunel restaurant attached. A little further along Bonhay Road, just past the station is a super Chinese takeaway. A few yards beyond there, an all-purpose corner shop. The station itself has the usual buffet facilities.

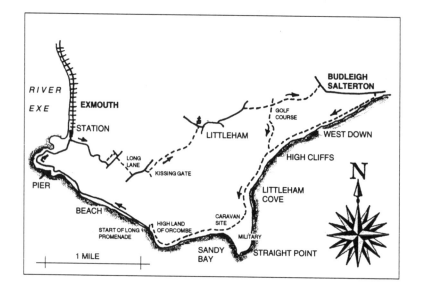

RIVER
EXE

EXMOUTH

STATION

LONG
LANE

KISSING GATE

PIER

BEACH

START OF LONG
PROMENADE

HIGH LAND
OF ORCOMBE

CARAVAN
SITE

SANDY
BAY

MILITARY

STRAIGHT POINT

1 MILE

LITTLEHAM

GOLF
COURSE

**BUDLEIGH
SALTERTON**

WEST DOWN

HIGH CLIFFS

LITTLEHAM
COVE

N

Walk 12
Exmouth Circular

A circular walk, with gently undulating Devon countryside on the outward leg, the South West Coastal Path for the return. This section is quite hilly, but the views are magnificent.

Starting Station: Exmouth
Distance: 10.5 miles (Shorter choice 8 miles)
Finishing Station: Exmouth
Map: 192
TIC: Alexandra Terrace, Exmouth, Devon, EX8 1NZ;
Tel 01395 263744
Problems: Two flights of unevenly spaced steps on the Coast Path can be awkward for anyone with dodgy knee joints.

The history of Exmouth is one of fashions. In the 17th century, it was popular as a place for Exeter people to bathe in the sea. With the Napoleonic Wars excluding early travellers from the continent, it became very fashionable. This lasted until the railway was built on the other side of the river in 1848. Its arrival gave easy access to the Torbay coast and Exmouth's popularity fell dramatically.

Several attempts were made to get the town connected to the railway system, but it was not until 1861 that this was achieved. By the turn of the century its renaissance had come. Family holidays were just starting to become popular and the bucket and spade era was beginning. Long sandy beaches encouraged that kind of visitor then; as it does today. A kind climate and enough buildings to make the place interesting without ever becoming overpowering keep Exmouth a very pleasant place to visit: for the day or an extended break.

Leave the station and cross the service road directly outside. Across is a sign, Subway To Town Centre. Take this and bear left with the road alongside The South Western Hotel into The Parade and towards a half-timbered building housing accountants and solicitors. This leads past No Entry signs into Albion Street. Halfway up the hill, take the right turn into Montpelier Road. At the end, turn the left – uphill – along Boarden Barn and first right into Raddenstile Lane.

As the road swings sharp right by the Holy Ghost Catholic Church, take the lesser road that continues straight on. At the end of the lane turn right to the a road. Directly across is a narrow lane that is forbidden to motor vehicles. This is Long Lane but unmarked, and is actually one of Devon's green lanes.

When this lane meets the main road turn left along Douglas Avenue. After some 300 yards, another green lane leads off to the right opposite Mayfield Drive. Almost immediately, another footpath sign points the way right. Ignore this; follow the path to Littleham. When this lane eventually turns sharp right, ignore the footpath to the left on the bend, walking a few yards further to an iron kissing gate on the left. This is the walk.

A narrow lane leads into a field. At this point, aim just to the right of a farm. This will lead through a gate and a stile past these buildings, across the farm drive and into another field. At the point where this field narrows, another gate on the left leads out of the field towards Littleham.

On meeting the road in the village turn right, past the church and first left into Castle Lane.

The church of St. Margaret and St. Andrew is the centrepiece of this village. Although heavily restored in 1884, much of the 15th century building remains, with a 13th century chancel. In the south-east corner of the churchyard can be found the grave of Lady Nelson, the widow of the Admiral whose exploits at sea were of the most gallant: more than can be said for his tangled personal life. She died in London in 1831, Horatio having predeceased her by some 26 years, but was interred in this rural county location. Her son Josiah and his chidren are also buried here.

The village has a post office and stores, opposite the church, a pub called The Clinton Arms selling Ushers beers and food, and toilets right on the corner.

Follow this country lane for something over half a mile. Rejecting the siren call of the right turn to Woodlands Farm, keep to the left of the thatched cottage there. Approaching a wooded area on the right, a Public Footpath to the right is the route of this walk. Ignoring several offshoots from this path, it will deliver you to hole number 7 of East Devon Golf Club; beware flying balls from the left.

Circle this to the right and follow the wider but lesser used track towards the left. The gravel path which may appear to be first choice only leads to the next tee. At the top of this track comes the parting of the ways. For the shorter walk, turn right, then across the golf course. The path climbs steadily until the effort is rewarded with a wonderful view out to sea. Turn right along the Coastal Path, and rejoin the walk description at *.

The longer walk, take the path almost directly ahead, over the golf course. This time, balls will arrive from the right. Exit at the gate and follow the clearly defined path across the next field. The views from here are extremely attractive. The cluster of buildings that will soon develop into Budleigh Salterton and rolling hills beyond, with the chasm that is the valley of the river Otter between. The coastline continues its sweep towards Sidmouth and Seaton.

Walk straight past the signpost indicating that you are walking towards the Coast path, and to a road. Turn right into the town of Budleigh Salterton.

There was a settlement on this site in 1210; then known as Saltre. Salt pans or 'salterns' were used here for centuries which would seem to go some way towards explaining the etymology of this place. It has long been popular with visitors, although the pebble beach does not make for much of a seaside type family holiday. It is a very genteel place with a high percentage of older residents. There is no harbour as such, but boats once sailed two miles up the Otter to East Budleigh. This became silted and by the 16th century was no more. Sir Walter Raleigh was born there in 1552.

Budleigh Salterton has seen its share of celebrities over the years. P G Wodehouse and Noel Coward were two, but perhaps the most famous was Sir John Millais who lived in The Octagon in Mackerel Square. In 1870, he painted that most evocative of works 'The Boyhood of Raleigh', the setting being the sea wall.

Also here, The Fairlynch Museum and Arts Centre charts local history, geology, and the railway (when it ran). It opens from Easter to October and at Christmas.

On reaching the seafront turn sharp right and follow that path along the shore and steadily uphill. There is another toilet block a few hundred yards along. The climb increases in severity before reaching West Down Beacon some 400 feet (130 metres) above sea level. On a clear day it is possible to see across Lyme Bay as far as Portland Bill. There is also a seat to help you recover from your exertions. Continue following the South West Coastal Path down the other side. Shortly, a track from the right brings in the shortened walk.

Occasionally, there is the sound of gunfire from over on the left. The land at Straight Point has been taken over by the Royal Marines for use as a rifle range. It's uncanny how the military generally seem to select the most picturesque areas of Britain for their games.

* Down the flight of steps and up the other side, the walk arrives in the middle of a huge caravan site. Walk straight across, up the slope at the other side, and a fairly well concealed signpost will indicate the route of the footpath to the right. This will lead to The Beachcomber Restaurant. Head to the left of this building, and the cliff-top path can then be seen again.

At the inland end of this caravan site is a huge tourist attraction, essentially for the kids, but with lots of 'grown-up' interest too. Known as The World of Country Life, it covers over forty acres, much of it under cover, There you can admire a range of vintage farm machinery, some super old cars, a craft studio, and restaurant. It's open from Easter to the end of October each year.

Beyond the caravan park, the National Trust owns The High Land of Orcombe through which the walk passes. At the far end the path enters a narrow way. At the end, take the left hand – paved – path which leads down to the seashore. Follow this around, right along the seafront into the dock area. By following the road around to the right hand side of the water you will eventually come out into Camperdown Terrace. At the end, turn left into Victoria Way, bear left at the end into Imperial Road, and the station is across the way.

Exmouth Harbour.

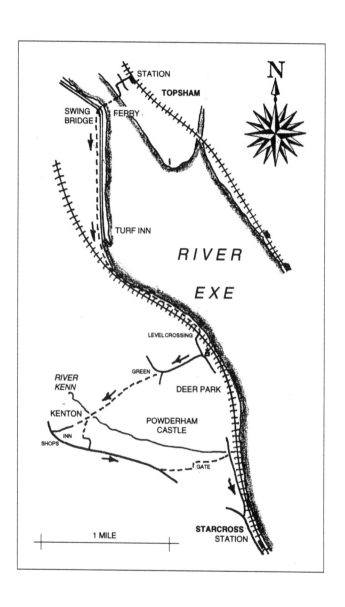

Walk 13
Topsham to Starcross

Which direction to walk this fasinating stretch was a dilemma not
entirely resolved. There are conflicting problems at each end. Is the
ferry running at Topsham? What time is the departing train at
Starcross? As they are few, it would be entirely possible to arrive at
Starcross with a wait of anything up to two hours. Or perhaps just take
pot luck and rely on the alternatives.

In the event, the ferry proved the more intractable, so that will be
used early on. By a large margin, this walk offers the biggest variety
of birds and mammals on any of these walks.

Starting Station: Topsham (Exeter to Exmouth line)
Distance: 6 miles
Finishing Station: Starcross (Exeter to Newton Abbot line)
Map: 192
TIC: Civic Centre, Paris Street, Exeter, Devon EX1 1JJ;
Tel 01392 265700
Problems: Only as noted above. For ferry information contact the
TIC.

Exactly how far back Topsham goes is still open to debate. There is a strong
body of opinion that there was a Celtic trading settlement here long before
the Romans established their port serving *Isca Dumnoniorum* (Exeter) here
early in the 1st century AD.

When they left, the name disappears from records, not to be heard of again
until Saxon times. Whether the place stayed in occupation is not known. We
do know that is was recorded in Domesday and that there was a salmon
fishery active.

The major event in its history was a long-running battle between Exeter
and the Courtenay family who were the Earl and Countess of Devon. Back

in 1282, Isabel ordered a weir to be built across the river at Topsham. This eliminated any chance of boats that by then were reaching Exeter, continuing to do so. Thus, Topsham, on land owned by the family, became the port for Exeter.

After a brief period, a small opening was cut in the weir, but the Earl of Devon blocked it again, withstanding many and varied efforts to remove it. His descendants continued to get rich by charging duty to use the Topsham quay. It was not until 1539 that the weir was removed. By then, the river was badly silted, and navigation was not possible.

The town/village/port itself is a collection of multi-hued houses. Many are built of Dutch brick, landed after being used as ballast by incoming ships. Much of the serge made in Devon was shipped through the port to Holland.

Now most of the evidence of its old status has gone. All the buildings connected with shipbuilding and its attendant trades have disappeared. The place is very much a dormitory town for Exeter, but still manages to retain most of its old character.

Arriving on the platform from Exeter, walk back to the main road, turn left over the level crossing and to the crossroads in town. Opposite, but slightly to the right is Follett Road. Follow this to the bottom and turn left into Ferry Road. The slipway for the ferry is on the right, some 200 yards along. If the ferryman is not there, you need to fetch him from home. It's only a few yards away, and directions are on the board outside the cabin.

The house on the right, just before the ferry is Follitt Lodge where Sir William Webb Follitt, a 19th century Attorney General, used to live. The Passage House Inn is just a few yards further along. Built in 1721, this fine old place sells Bass, and the local Heavitree beer.

At the other side of the river, cross the swing bridge over the canal and turn left down the towpath.

The Exeter Canal is generally accepted to be the first canal in England to use pound locks when the one-and-a-half mile canal opened in 1566. The corporation of Exeter engaged John Trew to make a canal alongside the river. He cut a channel 16 feet wide and three feet deep which passed boats of up to 16 tons, but also provided 'vertically rising sluices arranged in pairs'. There were three locks, and the line ran from close to the city wall in Exeter to just beyond the infamous Countess Weir, a name that has lasted to this day. Below, the river was improved allowing access to the new canal. The water for the canal came – as it does today – from the Exe via a weir close to the city.

Whilst this was considered a great improvement, it was a long way from being a satisfactory one. It was difficult to access when the tide was low, and silting eventually became a problem. During the Civil War, little was done to maintain the waterway, and trade was decreasing. Topsham Quay was still in use, which reduced the level of trade going through to the city.

Further improvements and lengthening took place between 1675 under Richard Hurd, and 1698 when the whole canal was enlarged to take boats of up to 140 tons. A new lock was also built under the direction of one Richard Bayley. Although the work was started by this gentleman, it was finished by local citizens after Bayley decamped suddenly. This improved navigation, but again, not by much. Bigger boats meant deeper draught, and they could still only reach the canal during spring tides.

It took over a century, the canal continuing in regular use, before any further improvements were made. It was then the turn of James Green. His association with the Exeter Canal began in 1818 when he was engaged to report on possible improvements. These suggestions were acted upon in 1820.

He was again consulted in 1824 to suggest ways of improving access, still difficult when tides were wrong. His proposal was to extend the canal southwards for two miles to Turf. From here, boats could access the lock at any state of the tide. He also proposed raising the bank to improve the depth, and construction of a basin in Exeter to avoid having to improve the river above the canal. The work started in 1825 and was finally completed when the new basin was ready for use in September 1830. The improvements he carried out left the line pretty well as we see it today. The only major change is the dereliction of the lock that gave access to the river at Topsham.

Open flood plains now predominate as the canal nears its end. There are moored boats above the sea lock, and a pub, The Turf, hard by. Whether this is a lonely abandoned outpost or vibrant centre of interest depends on whether you visit in summer or winter. The sea lock and landing stage below are all in full working order.

From here until the walk leaves the estuary, there is much bird life to see. The usual raucous collection of mallards and seagulls is augmented by several species of duck. Herons (frequently) and egrets (occasionally) also inhabit the waterside.

The path continues alongside the sea wall for well over a mile before arriving at a level crossing. Over the railway, turn left, and on reaching the road; turn right. The 15th century St. Clement's church is on the corner and worth a visit if the door is unlocked. Walk up the straight road until it turns to the right. Directly ahead, over the green is a Public Footpath notice and a gate. Follow this up the hill and down the other side into the valley of the river Kenn. Notice the high fencing to the left. This is the Powderham estate, and behind this you will see fallow deer belonging to the castle. It is extremely unlikely that you will miss them: there are some 700 in residence.

On crossing this river, there is a footpath sign pointing to the left. This leads to a road where another left turn will deliver you to the main road: but beyond the shops and pubs. To access these, continue up the narrow lane, past the pretty brook and out into the centre of Kenton.

There are two pubs in the village: The Devon Arms and The Dolphin Inn, both serving food. Together with a post office and village stores, you should find most of your needs catered for. The river Kenn used to be navigable up to the village, and a trade with France was under way in the 16th century.

'Dads Army' had a triumph here during the last war when a Luftwaffe pilot parachuted into the High Street. The Home Guard soon had him a prisoner.

Turn left and walk along the footpath. After about half a mile, the entrance to Powderham Castle is reached on the left.

The castle is open to visitors from Easter to the end of September. 'Castle' is something of a misnomer: fortified Manor would be more accurate. The estate has been in the Courtenay family since the early 14th century. The first building work on the site was started by Sir Philip Courtenay, Lord Lieutenant of Ireland at the end of the 1300s. It must have been quite a site in its heyday. Until 200 years ago, the Exe estuary washed the foot of the hill on which the castle is built.

During the Civil War a Royalist garrison was based here. The Round-heads under Fairfax attacked and were repulsed, falling back to St. Clement's church. The Crown forces then attacked that building, only to withdraw after the arrival of another force under the command of Sir Hardress Waller. The Castle finally surrendered shortly afterwards on 25 January 1646.

Major reconstructions took place at the beginning and end of the 1700s, including an embankment built to hold the estuary back to where it is now. The cupola on the hill to the north-west dates from this time. Today, the exterior is completely 1760 to 1860, but with some of the original work inside the walls.

The house is currently a family home to Lord and Lady Courtenay. He will become the 18th Earl of Devon upon the demise of his father. There are some exquisite treasures, paintings and furnishings, making a visit almost mandatory.

Continue up the footpath for another half mile. Here, on the right hand side is a pink cottage, and on the left opposite, a Public Footpath sign over a stile pointing left onto the park. Follow the fence around the perimeter of the field and at an iron kissing gate cross the track into another field. Again, stick to the left hand edge of the field and you will eventually reach a road with the railway and estuary just beyond. Turn right and follow this lane until it reaches the main road. Here, on the left, is a gate. Pass through this and head for the railway. A path leads alongside the tracks to Starcross station.

The Atmospheric Railway Inn lies very close to the station. About Starcross, there is little to say. It is no more than a pleasant collection of houses, originally promoted as a holiday spot. Having lost out to Dawlish in the race to attract visitors, it never grew.

If you arrive at the station with a very long time to wait for a train, or have to get back to Topsham, there is another option during the summer season. Alongside the station is a ferry which crosses the river to Exmouth, as it has done since the 12th century. The rail service from that town to Topsham and Exeter is far better. On reaching Exmouth, follow the instructions at the end of Walk 12 for a route from the docks to the station.

Dutch-style housing in Topsham.

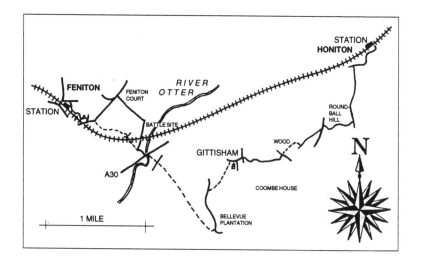

STATION
HONITON

FENITON

RIVER
OTTER

FENITON
COURT

STATION

BATTLE SITE

ROUND-
BALL
HILL

WOOD

GITTISHAM

N

A30

COOMBE HOUSE

1 MILE

BELLEVUE
PLANTATION

Walk 14
Feniton to Honiton

Delightful rather than dramatic would sum up this walk in the east of the county. No seascapes today, but the lush green rolling hills more than compensate.

Starting Station: Feniton
Distance: 7 miles
Finishing Station: Honiton
Map: 192
TIC: Dowell Street, East Car Park, Honiton, Devon EX14 8T;
Tel 01404 43716

The name *Feniton* has appeared on the station only in comparatively recent times. It was known as Sidmouth Junction when the line to that town opened in 1874, and changed after the branch was closed. The village itself is quite unimpressive; just an ordinary little village, now popular with Exeter commuters. There is some pleasant modern housing counterpointed by older ones, but with no real atmosphere. To a degree, the place is schizoid. The larger – and more modern – part is clustered around the station whilst Feniton Court, a fine Georgian mansion is surrounded by much older buildings, inevitably with more character. For instance, the 15th century church of St. Andrew's contains some compelling interior architecture.

|| Leave the station and turn right over the level crossing.

If you are already in need of liquid sustenance, The Dog Inn is just across the road from the station. There are shops in the first few yards over the railway.

|| Turn immediately right again into Station Road. Take the second on the right – York Crescent – and bear left with the road. Carry

straight on where the main road appears to go left and take the first left into Salisbury Crescent. This describes a large arc coming alongside the railway before meeting another road. Here, turn left and walk to the bend in the road where a Public Footpath sign indicates a path to the right.

A choice of route now. If you prefer to take in the church, Feniton Court and the battlefield – where there is nothing much to see:

Carry straight on up the road to the housing. Follow the more major of the roads to the right, past the church and continue under the railway, battlefield on the left, to meet up with the other route at *

A battle in the Western Rebellion was fought here at the end of July 1549, just a few days before the decisive one at Clyst Heath. The initial suppression of the monasteries by Henry VIII had little effect on this far corner of the kingdom. But the liturgical and doctrinal changes were felt when the Act of Uniformity was introduced in 1549. These were strongly resented locally. An uprising started on the north of Dartmoor, gathered pace through Crediton, and laid seige to Exeter. An army of mercenaries arrived from London were met here by some of that force. After a skirmish, the army moved to Exeter and the rebellion was crushed. The remnants of the uprising were followed home to Sampford Courtenay, captured and hung.

Following the Public Footpath route: Walk across a series of fields. At one stile, a Public Footpath arrow points left: ignore it and continue straight ahead until the path reaches a lane. Directly ahead is a barn. Turn left to the end of that building, turn right, walk across the gateway and down a narrow track alongside the white house to a stile giving access to the railway. Cross the line carefully, turn left and walk down alongside the track for a few yards to the stile on the right.
    In this field, keep left and the exit stile is a few yards along. Continue down the green lane to the road; turn right.

* At the main road, turn left, walk along, over the bridge spanning the river Otter and turn right into the Public Bridleway.

Extra care is needed on this short section; it is the busy A30 trunk road and carries a heavy volume of traffic. There is a wide verge as far as the bridge, but no footway over the water.

This bears left after a few yards – ignoring the footpath straight ahead, and continues as a green lane gently uphill. Cross the small road, pass through the gate and continue the climb. This is quite gentle by Devonian standards, although it lasts something around a mile.

As you climb, the views behind increase in beauty as the Otter valley become more dramatic. It is also a popular area for gliding. The North Hill club have their base across the far side, and soaring machines are frequently to be seen, sun glinting off their shining bodies.

Eventually, the track swings sharp left and meets a road. Turn left and drop down the hill for half a mile to a thatched cottage on the right. Alongside is a Public Footpath sign. In this field, keep the hedge to your left shoulder until reaching a metal gate. Pass through and continue, this time with the hedge to your right shoulder. Across the valley is a white house. Aim directly for that and a kissing gate will provide the exit to this field, over a wooden footbridge spanning a deep gully with a tiny stream in the bottom.

Turn left, still aiming for the house. Pass through another gate into a lane which duly arrives at Gittisham village green alongside the church.

Pretty thatched cottages in Gittisham.

91

Built predominantly from cob and thatch, Gittisham is one of the prettier villages visited during the course of these walks. What a shame the church lets it down; at least externally.

St. Michael's was constructed during the reign of Henry VII, but has been 'improved' over the centuries. The original thatched roof was replaced by slate in 1800, and the tower cement rendered. Inside, the almost Spartan image is continued. Some stained glass, box pews with very high sides and a gallery at the west end. The organ is hand pumped and has candleholders alongside the console.

The houses outside the church were originally part of a school. They were built in 1720 by Sir Thomas Putt who, reflecting the fact that Devon was ever a sea-going county, enjoined that the pupils be taught 'reading, writing, arithmetic, the catechisms and navigation.'

Two Silver Jubilees of King George V and Queen Elizabeth II are commemorated in the square by a tree and seat respectively.

In the village there is a shop that has half-days on Thursday and Saturday and does not open Sundays, and a Post Office.

Turn right at the end of the square and follow the road through the village. A pretty stream runs through the middle, crossed by an equally attractive bridge. The road again moves uphill, passing the entrance to Coombe House, once the local manor, now an hotel.

Almost a mile along, the road turns sharp right whilst the walk takes the track straight ahead through woods. On meeting the sign indicating no entry except to The Barn, turn right up to the road and turn left.

Walk along here until meeting a busier road and bear left. A short way down the hill, take the narrow lane on the right. This skirts Roundball Hill drops into a valley and crosses a stream. Turn left towards the outskirts of Honiton.

Immediately on the right is a very old orchard, its trees unpruned and apparently uncared for. In spring, the blossom is a picture; by late summer, the branches are laden with fruit.

Walk down this road to a T-junction, turn left and immediately right. At the end of this road turn right into Littletown Road. Follow the road around to the left as it becomes Marlpits Lane, past the timber yard on the left and a hospital on the right. At the end, turn left and the station's entrance is a few yards down on the left.

It's one of those word associations so beloved of the psychiatric profession. Say 'Honiton' and the response is sure to be 'Lace!' But there is more to the town than that. The main London to Exeter highway the A30 – which now mercifully bypasses the town – was a Roman road, linking Exeter with Watling Street. Honiton was the centre of the serge trade, weekly markets being held in the town. A major customer was Holland, and the serge was shipped out through Topsham – see Walk 13. There is little of antiquity in the town as the residents historically seem to have a propensity to burn the place down. Major fires were recorded in 1672, 1747, 1754 and 1765.

Prior to that, the town had impressed such luminaries as Daniel Defoe, author of Robinson Crusoe. As he first arrived at Honiton Hill, overlooking the town, he noted that '... it is the most beautiful landscape in the world ... and I do not remember the like in any one place in England.'

Honiton Lace has been manufactured since Elizabethan times; Queen Victoria's wedding veil was made here. It's a type of pillow-made bobbin lace. In 1698 there were 4,695 lace makers: today there are none. Although machine production killed the trade, there are still those in the town who have the necessary skills, and can turn out exquisitely beautiful work to special commissions. The Queen and the Speaker of the House of Commons have both received Honiton Lace in recent years.

The town is also known for glovemaking, and has a strong agricultural tradition. But the face of the place is still towards the old A30. A wide thoroughfare with all the architectural interest centred there. And, if you want to look at lace in all its beauty, there is the Allhallows Museum which has a collection representing production over the last 350 years, or the Honiton Lace shop where you can buy antique lace. Both these places are in the High Street.

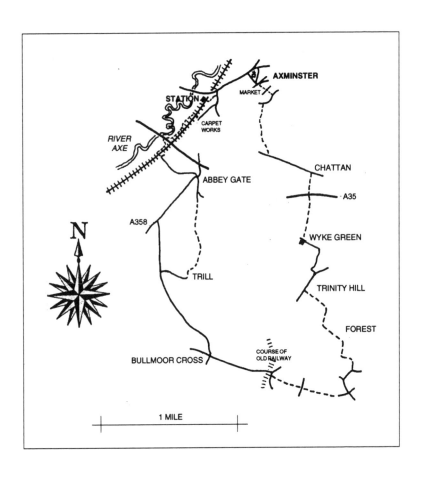

AXMINSTER

MARKET

STATION

CARPET
WORKS

RIVER
AXE

ABBEY GATE

CHATTAN

A35

A358

WYKE GREEN

TRILL

TRINITY HILL

FOREST

BULLMOOR CROSS

COURSE OF
OLD RAILWAY

N

1 MILE

Walk 15
Axminster Circular

About as far east as you can go and still remain in Devon. The scenery is still magnificent, and the town itself pleasant.

Starting Station: Axminster
Distance: 8 miles
Finishing Station: Axminster
Map: 193
TIC: The Old Courthouse, Church Street, Axminster, Devon EX13 5AQ; Tel 01297 34386
Problems: The first half of this walk is mostly uphill. None too steep, but uphill nevertheless.

Yet another place of great antiquity, Axminster sits on the top of a hill overlooking the river Axe. It was here that the Icknield Street and Fosse Way intersected, although there is no current evidence of Roman occupation. But there are indications of Saxon settlement in 670AD. Its name is self-explanatory: a minster was built here in the 8th century. The town was granted its Market Charter by King John in 1210, and an abbey at Newenham founded in 1246.

But the reason for the name of Axminster being so well known is its carpets. There was a carpet manufactory established in the town by Thomas Whitty in 1755. A weaver of cloth, he was the first person to achieve factory production of carpets, although the slow laborious process which involved much child labour was completely at odds with mass production techniques. Indeed, in the early days, the completion of a carpet was such a singular event that it was taken to church to be blessed, and the event celebrated by ringing of the church bells.

The business went bankrupt in 1835 and the looms were sold to Wilton (Wiltshire) which subsequently established its name as a maker of fine carpets. Another company re-established carpet making in Axminster in 1937, and have relocated to a factory near the station. The original building was demolished, but the one used at the restart is still standing. The company has a showroom, and it is possible to see some of the manufacturing in progress.

There are several other buildings of interest around the town; some aged, some not. Strangely, after the antiquity of some guildhalls in Devon, the Axminster one was built in 1931: as a cinema! In 1964, with the demise of Hollywood epics, it was converted for council use, and now features blood and thunder Town Council meetings.

The Old Court House was once the police station, but has transmogrified over the years to hold the TIC, a senior citizens cen-tre, council enquiry office, a museum and the Citizens Advice Bureau.

Leave the station and turn left. Follow the pavement, not the road, and this passes along a narrow walkway before reaching a traffic island. Straight ahead, up the hill into the town.

At the top, there is a right turn – Church Street – which gives access to the old court house, but the walk carries on for a few more yards into the shopping area before turning right past the church into Silver Street.

The minster church of St. Mary the Virgin was founded in 786 when Cynehard, an Anglo-Saxon prince was brought for burial. The church has been heavily rebuilt over the centuries but a Norman tower remains. The Yonge family, many of whom are buried in the church, were wealthy locals who lived in the Mansion House close by from 1450 to 1700. They added the south chancel aisle in about 1480.

At the end of here turn left. Immediately around the corner is a right hand fork with the cattle market and Coombe Lane Long Stay Car Park. Take this fork, and after only a few yards, turn right again alongside the market. This road peters out into a footpath which reaches a road. Straight across, up another path to the next road and turn right.

Some 70 yards along is a fire station on the left. Beyond is a Public Footpath sign. Take this. The path skirts a field with poultry in it and reaches a junction. Take the straight ahead track, over a brook and stile into a field. Keep to the right of this field, with tennis courts and housing at the other side of the hedge. At the exit to this field is a crossing of paths; keep straight on over further stiles and another concrete footbridge which gives access to another field. Here, bear slightly to the left, aiming to pass an electricity post to the left. This course will bring you to the stile at the end of this field.

Turn left and walk up the road for about half a mile to the crest of the hill. Turn right towards Kings Farm. This soon arrives at the Axminster bypass. The path heads left down into the cutting. Cross the road and take a small road almost opposite. As this reaches a cattle grid, there are some steps on the left to a stile. Cross this and aim towards the right hand edge of the coppice beyond and this will ensure a safe arrival at the next stile. Continue over a series of stiles until you enter the last field before a thatched white cottage straight ahead. The exit stile to this field is in the far left corner.

Turn left and follow this track uphill to a road. Turn right and some 300 yards along on the left is a wide entrance to the Forestry Commission land at Trinity Hill. Pass through the main gate and follow the drive, now in woodland. This bears to the right just before the next gate which is marked 'Private'.

The track continues to weave its way along a pleasant tree-lined walk to the next road. Here turn right and at the next junction, turn left to Uplyme. Some 400 yards along, take the Public Bridleway sign to the right. This lane leads into a field. Keep close to the hedge through this field. Cross a road and straight over the next field. At the next road, turn right.

This part of the walk is also used by The East Devon Way. Waymarked with a foxglove logo, this walk covers some 38 miles from Exmouth to Uplyme. It visits some beautiful villages and hamlets on the way, and can be turned into a 65 mile circular walk by heading from Uplyme into Lyme Regis and returning to Exmouth along the Coat Path – a section of which is used in Walk 12.

Only a few yards along here, the road – and this walk – turns sharp right. The wall here was once the parapet of a railway bridge.

The old railway line that ran from Axminster to Lyme Regis was quite short lived. Opened in 1903, the coming of the railways had the same effect on this Dorset town as it did on the Devon ones covered elsewhere in this book. It was a steeply graded line, had a large viaduct at Cannington, and was much loved by railway enthusiasts and photographers alike. One attraction for them – if not the average traveller – was the vintage carriages that were used there. Clean they may have been, but comfortable: no. The branch was worked by Adams-designed tank engines which arrived there in 1913 and never left. One clocked up a staggering 2,070,918 miles having spent 48 of her 76 year life on this line. Closure was effected in November 1965.

|| Follow this road, signed 'Musbury' to the next junction. Here, turn
|| right at Bulmoor Cross towards Trill.

May is an excellent time to consider this walk. The woodland areas are carpeted with bluebells, making it even more attractive than usual.

|| This road eventually reaches the main road. Turn right and con-
|| tinue to a house on the right called Abbey Gate House, 100 yards
|| before the Axminster bypass crosses overhead. Turn left here,
|| walk down the lane to the second farm and take a left to cross the
|| railway. Immediately, turn right and follow the path, detouring
|| briefly to go under the new road, close alongside the railway.
|| When the river closes in tight to the path, cross a bridge over a
|| tributary and an archway on the right is discovered. Go under this,
|| which used to bring the Lyme Regis branch into Axminster
|| station, cross the railway and take the path to the left, alongside
|| the carpet works. As this reaches a road, turn left. At the end turn
|| left again, and another path to the left soon returns the walk to the
|| station.

Walk 16
Tiverton Parkway Circular

A circular walk from Devon's newest InterCity station. Tiverton Parkway was built in the 1980s as a replacement for Tiverton Junction, which had become something of an anachronism after the closure of branches to Tiverton and Culmstock. Now, the station is strategically placed to tap trade both from the whole of north Devon, and the M5 which runs alongside. This walk has rather more than its fair share of roads. Not bad planning, but a country route that is walkable whatever the conditions underfoot is always useful. There are no flooded valleys or fields with bottomless bogs to impede this walk.

Starting Station: Tiverton Parkway
Distance: 6.5 miles : 7.75 with Detour – see text
Finish Station: Tiverton Parkway
Map: 181 and 192
TIC: Phoenix Lane, Tiverton, Devon EX16 6LU; Tel 01884 255827

Leave the station by the only road possible. As you reach a post with a huge sign atop carrying the BR logo, turn right, up the paved path to the main road and turn right. Cross the M5 roundabout and head towards the Little Chef. The first road to the right is a lane which also gives access to the Little Chef. Carry on down here, around a left bend, and 50 yards along is a green lane on the right which is the walk. At the end of this lane is a farm; bear left and walk to the road junction; turn right.

Across the road is the mile and a half mile diversion via Uffculme.

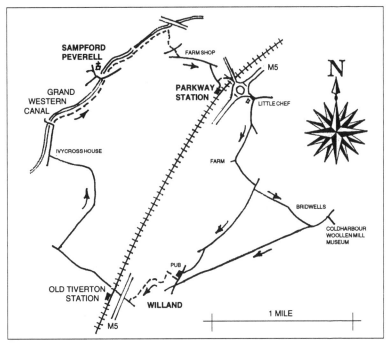

A fine pub and restaurant in Sampford Peverell.

DIVERSION ONLY: Walk down the lane almost directly across. This is a most delightful tree-lined avenue past the very ornate Bridwells. At the far end of this lane turn left and after 200 yards, a narrow lane leads off to the right. The entrance to Coldharbour Mill Working Wool Museum is at the bottom.

This fascinating evocation of Devonian times past is open throughout the year. The whole thing is a real hotch-potch of very attractive buildings, with displays and guided tours that are a fascinating introduction to this rural industry. Of particular interest to anyone with an engineering bent is an 1888 Lancashire boiler powering a 1910 Pollit and Wigzell steam engine. This is not always operational, so a call before visiting will confirm 'steam-up' times. There is a Mill Shop – of course – and a restaurant which serves cream teas.

DIVERSION ONLY: Walk back up the hill to the main road and turn left. Follow this road for 1.25 miles to a major crossroads. Turn right and take the lane to the left, just alongside the Halfway House.

MAIN WALK ONLY: Walk alongside the road for about a mile. Cross to the left hand side and, on reaching a parking area, take the old course of the road. This may appear to end after a few yards, but there is a clear path over the earth bank. This is merely a defence against New Age Travellers who were taking up residence here. On rejoining the main road, cross to The Halfway House pub, and turn right at the far end of the building.

The pub carries a splendid sign, decorated with a series of arrows indicating that it gets it name by being halfway between London and Penzance (160 miles), Taunton and Exeter (16 miles) Bridgwater and Exmouth (26 miles) and Plymouth and Bristol (60 miles). You can take a three-course Sunday lunch for £5.50, and consume Usher's famed west country brew. The garage next door has a shop which sells the basic snacks and drinks always needed on a walk like this.

Walk down the lane for some 250 yards, past a very attractive thatched cottage and to a gate on the left with a Public Footpath sign. Take this, across the stile into the next field and at the far end, on the right, is another stile. Cross this and turn immediately left over a scaffolding footbridge. This leads along the back of an industrial estate, past a building marked Excel Logistics to a road. Straight across, a few yards up a concrete road is another track which leads to another road; turn right.

A few yards to the left is a fish and chip shop, albeit with somewhat restricted opening hours.

This is Station Road. Walk under the motorway and railway bridges. Tiverton Junction station used to be on the left here. Follow this road for about half a mile to a right turn marked Sampford Peverell. This narrow lane winds its way to a junction at Ivyhouse Cross. Turn right and after a few yards the road bears left, up a rise and to a bridge. Turn right onto the Grand Western Canal towing path.

As you head for the towpath, notice the lumps of stone set into the edge of the road on the bridge. This is to deflect wheels before they make contact with the brickwork. The Grand Western Canal was one segment of a grand scheme to link the Bristol and English Channels. It was to run from the river Exe above Exeter to Taunton, there to make an end-on junction with the Bridgwater and Taunton Canal which had a link with the river Parrett. There would be three branches, including one to Tiverton which would run to that town from Burlescombe. Work on the highest level started in 1810, and four years later the main line from Lowdwells to Burlescombe and all the Tiverton branch was open.

The aim was simple. This was easy construction with no major engineering works, and there was limestone to be quarried alongside that could be carried by barge into Tiverton, there to be burnt in kilns for fertiliser. This would create an income from tolls that would fund further work. In the event it was almost a quarter of a century before the section to Taunton was completed and the southern extension was never built. This new section was one continual headache for the proprietors. They had recruited a local engineer, James Green, to complete the task. He was a believer in tub boat canals; small craft carrying some five tons.

This meant that instead of expensive locks which needed plenty of water, Green could build inclined planes and boat lifts to change levels. These constructions were always failing, and Green himself was dismissed before the project was completed. Indeed, by the time the connections were made, railways were starting to invade the area. A mere 31 years after completion, the Taunton section was abandoned, leaving just the original 11 miles still with that original trade: limestone.

The Great Western Railway bought the canal in 1864 and presided over its decline until a serious leak in 1924 gave them the excuse to close it. The canal festered away until a renewed interest in the 1960s saw the Devon County Council take over management in 1971, renaming it a Country Park. They have steadily refurbished the whole line and its towing path. It is possible to boat and walk the whole length. Bird life is abundant. There are ducks, coots and waterhens on the water and, if you are lucky, herons alongside. With a whole range of hedgerow birds along the towpath, it's an ornithologists delight.

The path soon leads to Sampford Peverell. It is possible to leave the towing path here, by the main bridge, to access two pubs.

The Globe is on the left and serves Whitbreads Ales. The Merrimeade Hotel is an altogether more grand affair. The bar offers a good range of real ales, and the restaurant is locally well known for the quality of its meals. The place has a Les Routiers listing and has been awarded three crowns by the English Tourist Board. The church of St. John the Baptist to the left of the canal is worthy of a closer look. There are several antiquities inside, but from the exterior, its squat tower gives an air of austerity that is does not deserve. Alongside, The Old Rectory was built in 1500 by Margaret Richmond Darby as a school of St. John the Baptist and was restored in 1850. The motto of the school was 'Learn to Do Well.'

Beyond the village, the canal carries on heading generally northeast. On reaching a large new road bridge, take the gate to the right hand side and walk down that path to the road. Straight across is a narrow lane which, after a few yards arrives at a T-junction. Turn left for the station.

On the left, walking back to the station is Little Turberfield Farm Shop. Unlike so many, this is a real one, selling much of their own produce. Lamb and beef is grown by the owner, who, guaranteeing to use no growth hormones, produces meat of real old-fashioned flavour and texture. And if taste is what you're after, try some local cider: Sheppey's Farmhouse from Milton Abbott, and Englefield Toe Kurler, made at Bradford-on-Tone. A super range of elegant jams and pickles grace the shelves along with greengrocery. Salcombe ice cream is another treat. The floor behind the counter slopes off at a crazy angle; if you've had any of their potent cider, you'll swear it has already taken effect.

The place is open from 8am to 5pm Tuesdays to Saturdays and comes very well recommended.

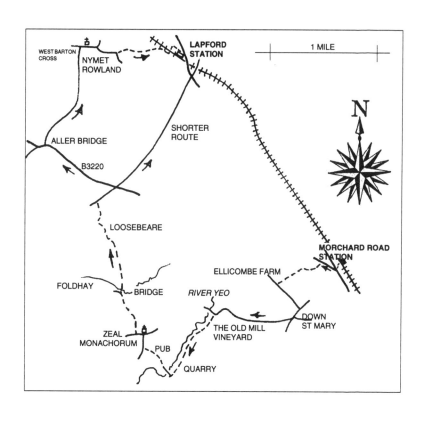

WEST BARTON CROSS
NYMET ROWLAND
LAPFORD STATION
1 MILE
SHORTER ROUTE
ALLER BRIDGE
B3220
N
LOOSEBEARE
MORCHARD ROAD STATION
ELLICOMBE FARM
FOLDHAY
BRIDGE
RIVER YEO
DOWN ST MARY
ZEAL MONACHORUM
PUB
THE OLD MILL VINEYARD
QUARRY

Walk 17
Morchard Road to Lapford

Some of the places we will reach during this walk are on the outer limits of the known universe: places Sir Ranulph Feinnes has yet to discover. To achieve a railway walk at all in this delightful uplands area demands careful planning. There are stations aplenty, although an infrequent service makes things awkward. But with perseverance and a timetable you will succeed: and be glad you did. No towns – hardy any villages for that matter; this is remote bucolic Devon at its very best, seemingly a million miles away from the places tourists normally reach.

Starting Station: Morchard Road (Exeter/Barnstaple)
Distance: 8 miles
Finishing Station: Lapford (Exeter/Barnstaple)
Map: 191
TIC: Market Street Car Park, Market Street, Crediton, Devon EX17 2BN; Tel 01363 772006
Problems: A couple of places (at least) are trying to reroute footpaths through their land. Rights of Way will not be extinguished, but some descriptions given may subsequently change. This will not affect the overall integrity of the walk.

The station at Morchard Road used to be the scene of an unusual activity. For many years, an overnight cabin was provided for a postman. He used to arrive with the mails from Winkleigh in time for the last train in the evening, and then retired to a bed, awaiting the first service next morning which conveyed his incoming mail.

For several years, Morchard Road station had an unlikely claim to fame:

Opposite: A pretty little footbridge near Zeal Monachorum.

it was quoted nationally as the *only* rail station on the Two Moors Way. This is a 100 mile footpath that links the only National Parks in southern England, Dartmoor and Exmoor. Starting in Ivybridge, near Plymouth, the Way crosses Dartmoor at its bleakest before descending into the lush green valleys of the county. At the northern end, it passes briefly into Somerset before finishing on the seashore at Lynmouth.

Sadly, events have overtaken that moment of national fame. Regional Railways have recently reopened a station at Ivybridge, close to the site of the earlier one; now there are two stations on the Way.

The actual village of Morchard Bishop is a hilly three miles away to the north-east. When the line was originally built there really was no alternative to following the Taw and Yeo valleys. Settlements tended to be further away on higher ground away from potential flooding, so whilst there are few railside villages, there are several smaller ones spread around the site of each station. Interestingly, all the stations that were built when the line opened almost a century and a half ago are still open.

Leave the station across the courtyard and, at the main road, take the Winkleigh road directly opposite. Some 300 yards along, a gate and cattle grid on the left give access to Ellicombe Farm. Cross another cattle grid, pass the houses and keep to the left of a barn into a rutted lane to a junction. Turn left and 50 yards on the right is a metal gate and a yellow footpath arrow. Cross the field up the hill until you reach the narrow lane; turn left into Down St. Mary.

This is a pretty little village in the best Devonian tradition. It's fairly quiet, not being on the road to anywhere, and has a good selection of cob and thatch cottages. The church is – of course – St. Mary's, and shows three distinct ages. The only bit of the original 12th century building is the tympanum over the south door; in place but well eroded by the weather. The original tower was destroyed in a hurricane at the start of the 1400s, and its replacement was built then. The body of the church was rebuilt in 1871. Particularly noteworthy inside are the pretty carvings on the pew-ends.

Walk straight through the village and keep to the right at a fork beyond the church, following the signs for 'Zeal Mnchm'.

On the edge of the village, to the right and set back from the road is an old Devonian Long House. It appears to be under restoration as the rounded south end is newly thatched whilst the rest has a corrugated iron roof – the standard old remedy for replacing thatch. A long house was just that, but the reason was that the farmer shared his accommodation with the livestock. The higher portion was for himself, the rest for animals.

⫶ Continue down the lane into a valley. On reaching a bridge, The
Old Mill is on the left. Turn up the drive and the footpath passes
to the left of the beautifully thatched house.

Over the centuries, this mill has been associated with fruit juices. Cider was
once made here, but its latest incarnation is as a vineyard. Carol and Simon
Pratt have established a good reputation locally for fine white wines. Only
planted in 1986, there are now some 4,000 vines in production. The product
is on sale and there is wine tasting. But be warned: If you taste you'll surely
buy, such is the quality. One customer gained that way is an establishment
that supplies drinks to many discerning and noble palates: The House of
Lords.

If you visited the church in Down St. Mary you will doubtless recognise
the bottle's label. It is a drawing of the pew ends. The owners are always
happy to talk to visitors about growing and production: well worth a stop.

The Down St. Mary Vineyard and Winery is open 11.30am to 5.30pm
Tuesdays to Saturdays, 12noon to 3pm Sundays. Further details on 01363
82300.

⫼ The path leads over a stile, across fields and along a bosky valley.

Keep an eye open along this section for wild life, particularly deer and foxes.
Often the best place to see them will be on the skyline. There is also plenty
of bird life. The name of this river may be a little confusing, as it clearly runs
north, but the Yeo that joins the Exe at Cowley Junction near Exeter runs
south. Strange though it may seem, there are two rivers of the same name.
They rise within a few hundred yards of each other, but on opposite sides of
the watershed. The southern one runs east through Crediton to the Exe. This
one empties into the Taw north of Nymet Rowland. An if that isn't enough
cause for bafflement, the second river crossed on Walk 20 in Barnstaple is:
the Yeo. Apart from sharing names, they also contribute jointly to the woes
of railway operation. In times of heavy rainfall, they can flood the tracks and
cause service cancellations. The name is believed to be a west country
corruption of the old English word for river: *eo*.

⫼ Stay generally close to the Yeo. Cross a stream and move out of the
woodland and slightly away from the river. This leads through an
apparently derelict quarry to a bridge over the river. Turn right
and walk up the hill, past the Waie Inn with a sports and
LeisureCentre, into Zeal.

Zeal Monachorum is unlike so many pretty Devonshire villages in that its population is declining. The 1831 census lists over 700 souls; this had dropped by two-thirds by 1961, but increased slightly to its current figure of some 300. Despite that, there is a super community spirit in the place, with several very active local organisations.

The buildings are mostly cob and thatch, the church a mainly 14th century structure, although the inside has been systematically 'modernised' – a euphemism for vandalised – by the Victorians. There is an ornate wooden seat with canopy outside the churchyard, part of the Silver Jubilee celebrations in 1977.

Turn right and walk towards the church. Beyond, turn left at the first junction signposted North Tawton. Immediately is a right turn to East Foldhay. Walk up this lane until you reach the end of the housing.

Pause awhile and look around. Over your left shoulder is Dartmoor, whilst directly ahead the hills of Exmoor can be seen.

The lane narrows and drops steeply downhill to a small bridge. Turn right just before it and walk alongside the water for a few yards, cross a sweet little ancient bridge and turn left, walking up the hill towards Loosebeare, mentioned in Domesday. Beyond the buildings, the main track turns right, whilst the walk follows a green lane almost directly ahead. At the end of this lane, turn right, and at the main road turn left.

At this junction, there is the option to shorten the walk by something over a mile. Walk straight across and follow the road to Lapford. At the main road, turn left and the station is 200 yards along on the left.

Follow this road for almost a mile before turning right by the chapel at Aller Bridge. At the top of this lane turn right at West Barton Cross, past the old church of St. Bartholomew into Nymet Rowland. Follow the main road through the village to the far end. Here the road swings sharp right and an unmade track – the walk – goes straight ahead, the cottage on the corner is called Far View.

Walk down this lane through a farmyard. Use the gate to the left hand side of the barn and follow the track. As this starts downhill, the obvious route is ahead and to the left, but the – unmarked

– path goes right through a gate and alongside the hedge into another field. Here, bear half right, down the hill to a stile. This brings the path alongside the railway. Cross a stile and at the end of that lane, a bridge takes the path to the left hand side of the track. As the path turns left, a kissing gate gives access to Lapford station platform.

The factory site across the line beyond the bridge was where the famed Ambrosia Creamed Rice pudding was made. The works was established in 1928. Other products included condensed milk, butter and Devonshire cream, drinking chocolate and yeast extract. The milk came from local farms on a fleet of 20 lorries – this was still the day of the milk churn – and by rail; almost 200,000 gallons in 1932. The firm moved to bigger and better premises, and closed their Lapford operation in 1970.

One oddity at Lapford, repeated at several other of the small stations on this line, was that there used to be a slaughterhouse alongside the railway. Here it was located under the arch at the south end of the platform. Similar small outfits were set up at Copplestone, Morchard Road and Eggesford. There are also cattle pens at every station along the line, as live animals were shipped by rail in the days before universal road transport. It was by no means a rare event for a complete farm to be moved: livestock, implements the family and their possessions, quite an organisational headache for the station-master and his staff.

The layout of this station, in the days when there were two platforms, was peculiar. The platform in use today was the 'up' – Exeter – one. For the 'down' line, the platform was at the other side of the road bridge. This is not unusual in itself, but the arrangements were. Passengers joined the stopping train at the factory side of the platform, and a separate track diverting off the down line was laid. The back of the platform was fenced so that down trains could not stop and unload whilst on the main line.

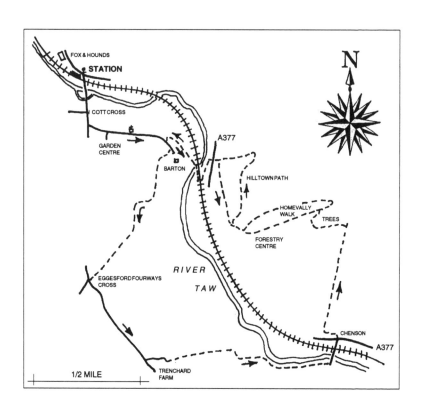

FOX & HOUNDS

STATION

N COTT CROSS

GARDEN CENTRE

BARTON

A377

HILLTOWN PATH

HOMEVALLY WALK

TREES

FORESTRY CENTRE

EGGESFORD FOURWAYS CROSS

RIVER

TAW

CHENSON

A377

TRENCHARD FARM

N

1/2 MILE

Walk 18
Eggesford Circular

For our next foray along The Tarka Line, we are using a section of The Tarka Trail. This is a 180-mile Devonian 'figure-of-eight' long distance footpath that extends from Exmoor and the Bristol Channel in the north to Dartmoor in the south. It was created under the auspices of Devon County Council in the mid-1980s and has used several sections of abandoned railway line in its length. Walk 20 will also use some of this Trail. On the ground, it is only discreetly marked; with a small disc bearing an otter's pawprint, usually affixed to a gate post. There is also a choice of distances here. A walk through The Forestry Commission's land at Eggesford can be as short as three miles. Full details in the text.

The unusual name comes from the Anglo-Saxon name *Egesa* – a common name in those times. Here, clearly, was his ford.

Starting Station: Eggesford on the Exeter to Barnstaple line
Distance: 3, 4 or 6 miles
Finishing Station: Eggesford
Map: 191
TIC: Market Street, Crediton, Devon EX17 2BN; Tel 01363 772006

Arriving from the Exeter direction, turn right at the exit. From Barnstaple direction, turn right, and right again over the level crossing. Cross the river Taw and walk up the road, past Cott Cross and take the next left marked 'Eggesford Gardens Entrance.'

Follow this road past the Garden Centre, the church and the gateway to Eggesford Barton until you reach a divergence of the paths.

Eggesford Garden Centre is a useful stopping-off point for refreshment. The walk returns this way, so it can be used as pre-walk fortification, or post-walk resuscitation as the need arises. The tea room offers a good range of simple foods with, inevitably, a Devon cream tea.

There is no village of Eggesford as such, but in the 13th century, a family called the Reigneys built their mansion with a church attached. After several rebuilds and changes of family fortunes, the house was finally demolished by the Earl of Portsmouth in 1832, and relocated across the valley.

The church has an interesting history, inextricably linked with local nobility. As an estate chapel, only seating 80 worshippers, the exterior of the building is quite ordinary. The tower, holding three bells is original 14th century, but the rest of the building and its interior were almost completely refurbished in 1878. Nevertheless, the inside is packed with memorials to successive generations. They are all around, decorated with coats-of-arms and really enliven the building. As you enter through the north door, The Portsmouth Pew is a box where the choir now sit. The organ, a single keyboard instrument made by Thomas C Lewis of London, installed in 1948 is also located there. Note the two foot pedals which activate the bellows.

Just outside the front corner of this pew is a pot-bellied stove, still plumbed in, that provided the Earl and his family with warmth during winter services. Electricity was not installed until 1965.

At this fork, decisions have to be made. The full length walk leads off to the right. For a shorter walk just using the forest area, take the left track, pass through a gate, cross the river alongside the railway and follow the waymark arrow to the road. There, straight across, is the entrance to Eggesford Forest. 100 yards along, take the right track which leads to the Information Centre and toilets. From there, two circular walks through the woodland are available. Their routes are marked by large posts, colour banded. The main walk will rejoin at *

Taking the right hand track, follow the lane to the fence at Eggesford Barton and turn right. Follow the path and cross the next stile. Pause here, looking to the right, and on the hill, plainly visible is the ruin of Eggesford House.

This once magnificent building, variously dated between 1820 and 1830 was home to the Portsmouth family until 1911. During that time, one of the daughters married Augustus Christie, owner of Tapeley Park, Instow (on the north coast of the county) whose son John, was the founder of Glyndebourne Opera House in Sussex.

Abandonment of Eggesford House was a tragedy. The family moved away to their Hampshire estate in 1913, offering Eggesford House and estate for sale. The House found no takers, but some of the associated buildings – the Fox and Hounds hotel on the main road for instance – were sold. The shell was just left after having all it interior fittings removed and sold.

It was constructed on a grand scale. There were 6 reception rooms, 30 bedrooms, domestic offices, servants quarters, stabling for 40 horses, but only 2 bathrooms; clearly personal hygiene was not quite as advanced in those days. The kitchens were supplied from walled gardens that covered over 3 acres.

Today, all that is remains is the crumbling shell. Future generations will reflect on the tragedy of this abandonment.

Continue up the path, following the line around the edge of a field, eventually arriving at Eggesford Fourways Cross. Turn left along the lane and continue until Trenchard Farm appears on the left. Turn down the drive, following the paved surface. Ahead is a barn, take the path to the right of that which leads to a gate and a green lane beyond.

Follow this path down, bearing left where the path splits, through another gate into a field. Turn right and follow the perimeter of this field around, alongside a tiny stream until a Public Footpath sign points right across the water and towards a gate alongside the river Taw.

The Taw is the principle river of north Devon, rising on Okemont Hill on Dartmoor. It then flows some 50 miles to join the river Torridge and the sea. Several smaller rivers feed it, most notably the Mole which rises on the edge of Exmoor, flowing south before entering the Taw at Kings Nympton, a few miles to the north of Eggesford.

Popular with sportsmen, it carries a good run of salmon and sea trout in season, some beats around the Eggesford area regularly producing fine catches.

Across the next field, the path leads to a narrow lane. Turn left, cross the river bridge and railway at Chenson Crossing. Beyond is the main road. Cross this, turn right and immediately left is a new pathway. Take this and turn left again after only a few yards. There is then a walk of some 50 yards to another fork in the track, either side of an electricity pole. Take the right hand – lesser used – one.

Follow this up the hill, through a gateway, always keeping the hedge to your left shoulder. As the gradient eases, there is a stand of trees on the left with a gap in the hedge. This leads into the woods, along a track to the edge of them. Follow this track as far as it goes and then turn right. Along here is another track to the right which leads back into the woods. Follow this down to the main track.

Here, the choices multiply. A left takes the walk to the Information Centre and toilets, whilst a right takes the walk to the Information Centre and toilets! But by the circuitous route; about half a mile longer. These all follow the blue posts of the Homevalley Walk. On reaching the Centre, all the walks join up.

The Forestry Commission was formed in 1919 as a government agency to take over, manage and initiate woodland planting schemes. Much early work has been criticised in recent years because of their obsession with planting non-indigenous but fast growing conifers. This policy is long past, and they are now sympathetic cultivators of English woodlands, very aware of their responsibilities to the environment and sensitive to the fact that they own vast tracts of countryside. This is manifested by a (relatively) recent policy of positive encouragement to visitors by waymarking walks around their woods.

The woodland on the Eggesford estate was one of their first acquisitions, and the very first tree under the régime was planted on 8 December 1919. Then, their one millionth tree was planted in Hilltown Wood in 1956

* From the Centre, follow the Hilltown (red marked) path. After only a few yards, take the lesser track to the right, up the hill. On reaching the outer edge of the woodland, the track will turn almost back on itself to re-enter the trees. That path leads to a main track; bear right. As the walk again reaches the edge of the woodland take the sharp left turn into the trees. At the next junction, the red posts lead to the left over a bridge. Follow the straight on path which gains the main road.

(If you took the short walk, the following is simply a return of that route)

Directly across the road is a Public Footpath sign, over a stile and pointing half left over a field towards a low railway overbridge. Under the railway, turn right, and up to the railway to cross the Taw. This path then leads back to the edge of Eggesford Barton, to return by the same way.

One benefit of using Eggesford station is that, even today, every train that uses the Tarka Line calls there. Whilst this may have something to do with the fact that it is the only section of double track between Crediton and Barnstaple, where trains can meet and pass, this was not always the case.

When the Earl of Portsmouth gave permission for the railway to be built, one of the conditions he imposed was that all trains were to stop at his private station. He also insisted that the company planted a screen of rhododendron bushes alongside the line so that Third Class passengers could not look into his estate.

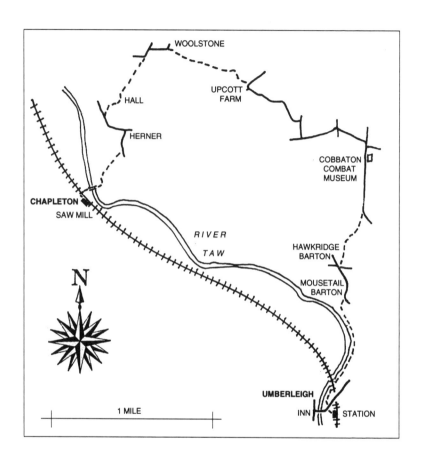

Walk 19
Chapelton to Umberleigh

Lots of ups and down on this walk, which takes in the lush greenery of the Taw valley and north Devon at its best.

Starting Station: Chapelton – Exeter-Barnstaple line
Distance: 5 miles
Finishing Station: Umberleigh
Map: 180
TIC: Tuly Street, Barnstaple EX31 1TY; Tel 01271 385583
Problems: Both stations are request stops. Tell the guard where you want to get off, and make sure that the driver can see you when you are waiting for the return train.

Chapelton is nothing more than a cluster of houses which never really justified a station. Although an average of 40 passengers a day used the station in 1930, it had dropped to as little as five by the mid-1970s. The fact that it only has three trains each way now does not help. Freight received a huge boost here in 1930 when Chappell and Watson opened the sawmills alongside and despatched a wagon a day with their finished products. Taken over by Rawle Gammon and Baker in 1966, the place is still active today, although the freight siding has gone, and everything moves by road. The station itself has been variously spelt Chapelton, Chapletown, and Chappletown in print over the years.

One small point of interest is that as you leave the platform, look across to what used to be the Up side and, behind the garden fence is an old station sign in Southern Railway malachite green: majestic when compared with the tinny white objects currently in use.

||| Walk to the north end of the platform and turn right, over the rails past the old station house. Through the gate, across the field and

river bridge, bear left and there is a clear track. Follow this to the lane at the end and turn left.

This leads to the hamlet of Herner. Turn left at the junction and follow the road for some 300 yards. Here, a wide track leads to the right off up the hill. This arrives at a meeting of the ways – all unsurfaced. If you turn right, there are two tracks together; take the left, up the hill. The other one passes between two iron gateposts and over a cattle grid. Follow the main track, first left, then right, into the courtyard of Hall,

This was the seat of the Hall family up to the 15th century. Then, one daughter married into the Chichester's of Raleigh to form yet another branch of this sprawling Devonian family. The gateposts outside the house give the identity away: a stone heron with an eel in its mouth. This house, although in the Elizabethan style, only dates back to 1850

Beyond Hall, the track continues to rise – much less steeply – before reaching a road. Actually, the road appears to join the track from the left; the walk is straight ahead. After only a few yards of road, take a right signed Woolstone. This is surfaced, but shortly turns left into the farm, leaving a deeply rutted track ahead for the walk downhill in what is now a green lane with high Devon banks. At the bottom the lane crosses a pretty stream on a little stone bridge.

Here is an strange piece of apparatus. Looking like a letter box, it is actually a pheasant feeder. Little slits in the drum allow the corn to fall through in a very controlled way.

Beyond, the lane climbs out of the valley, giving splendid views towards the south over the Taw valley.

Here is a very clear example of why walking in Devon can be such fun. A few minutes ago, the walk was a thoroughly intimate affair, deep in a valley with trees and water. At the top, it's stark, expansive and almost a different world.

The lane reaches Upcott farm; turn right. Follow this alleged road around its twists and turns to a junction. Turn right, and left at the bottom of the hill. This leads down into a valley at Chuggaton Cross, and up the other side. At the next junction, turn right and pass The Cobbaton Combat Collection.

This was opened in 1980 as a tourist attraction. The owner, Preston Isaac, had collected military ephemera since he was a child, and as he grew older, the size of his purchases grew; storing a 44 ton tank became quite a of problem. Eventually, he decided to share his hobby with others. What had started with a few bullet cases and belt buckles has become a comprehensive exposition of wartime equipment and armoured vehicles.

This is very much a hands-on museum with exhibits still in battle condition carrying damage they sustained in service: certainly not cleaned and polished. Originally, Preston's interest was in Second World War items, mainly British and Canadian. Now he has diversified into current equipment and post-war Russian and Czechoslovakian armoured vehicles. The replica Horsa glider on display was actually used in filming 'A Bridge Too Far'. There are Chieftain, Churchill Centaur and T54 tanks, armoured personnel carriers, guns, motor bikes, and scout cars; the makings of a good old trip down Memory Lane.

Basic refreshments are available. They are served, in keeping with the tenor of the place, from a 1940 Fordson 'V' NAFFI truck. The Cobbaton Combat Collection opens from 9.30am to 6pm every day from 1 April to 31 October, and 9.30am to 4pm 1 November to 31 March on weekdays only. Preston and his equipment were both in demand during 1995 as the 50th anniversary of VE Day approached.

Continue along the road up the hill. Over the crest, a gate on the right leads steeply down a field to a footbridge over Hawkridge Brook just to the right of the farm buildings. Turn right through the orchard and back up the field aiming slightly right of centre. At the top, a gate leads into the road.

Directly opposite a lane, signposted Umberleigh, leads away downhill. Follow this, past Mousetail Barton, for about 500 yards. As the road becomes an S-bend, there is a green lane leading off to the right with a Public Footpath sign. Take this, cross the stile and turn left, heading down towards the river. A path leads over a couple of stiles and under the railway bridge coming out alongside a factory owned by Murch Brothers, agricultural machinery people. On reaching the road, turn sharp left, and the station entrance is a few yards along on the right.

Although very small, Umberleigh's roots are firmly planted in the good soil of English history. In 936, King Athelstan built a palace at Umberleigh Barton. Rebuilt and altered over the years, in this century an engraved stone was found during work.

I John of Gaunt do hereby give to thee and thine
From me and mine
The barton fee of Umberlee
And so the world may know its truth
I hereby seal it with my tooth.

And he did! Although the stone is undated, John of Gaunt's life spanned the period 1340 to 1399. He became Duke of Lancaster in 1362, and was a distinguished soldier in the Hundred Years War.

Again, the justification for a station here originally must have been very little. In its heyday it handled only a few more passengers than Chapelton, and less freight, with the exception of livestock. The pretty station buildings on a gentle curve were aesthetically pleasing, and amongst the curios was a camping coach. These were provided by most of the railway companies at selected locations, and were old carriages converted for holiday use, something like a caravan. This one was first located in the 1930s, and not used after the war, although it was still on site in 1960.

The small church near Chapelton.

Now the whole area is derelict. All the buildings on the Up platform have been demolished, and trains stop on what was the Down side with only a 'bus-style shelter against the weather. The buildings here have been sold for a private house, but even in this quaint backwater, there is an intriguing wartime story.

After the evacuation of Dunkirk in 1940, thousands of servicemen were brought by train to army camps near Okehampton. Because of a severe lack of storage space locally where they would be relatively safe from bombing, the empty coaches were brought to Barnstaple. To store them, the 'Up' line as far as Umberleigh was closed, and single line working introduced. The closed line then became a six mile long siding. As the arriving coaches were checked, ammunition, guns and sundry other pieces of equipment were discovered. And Dunkirk sand! Our army's last foothold on continental Europe eventually found its way onto the ticket office desk in the station. What a shame Preston Isaac – from the museum up the road – hadn't started his collection then.

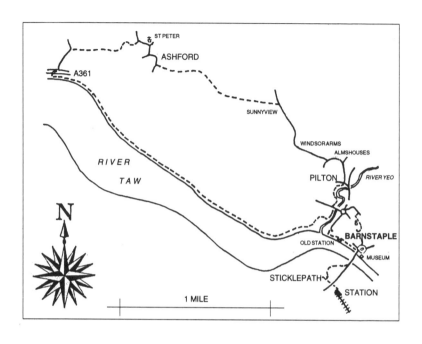

Almshouses in Pilton (photograph by Alison Fowler)

Walk 20
Barnstaple Circular

There is not much urban walking in north Devon, but this one does offer the chance to look around the pretty market town of Barnstaple. In medieval times, the major community was Pilton. This was because the hills along the Taw estuary made it defensible. Barnstaple was only a settlement at the lowest fordable point on the river. For the etymologically inclined, the crossing point was marked by a post: a stapol, placed by local resident Bearda. This walk visits Pilton and gives some magnificent views over the Taw estuary.

Starting Station: Barnstaple
Distance: 7.5 miles
Finish Station: Barnstaple
Map: 180
TIC: Tuly Street, Barnstaple EX31 1TY; Tel 01271 388583

Leave the station building and turn left towards the road bridge. Pass under, and at the gate take the right path. This describes a large arc before returning to the main road; turn left, over the town bridge.

This was the course of the old railway that once reached Ilfracombe. It saw many famous trains in its day; the *Atlantic Coast Express* and the *Devon Belle* used this section. The line crossed the Taw alongside but to the left of the road bridge with a flange-squealingly sharp turn needed to gain Town station. The section was closed on 20 October 1970.

The road bridge is believed to date from around 1200. Stone built, it was made up of 16 arches with spans of up to 22 feet, but was only about 9 feet wide; suitable for pedestrians and pack horses only. Widening took place in 1796 and 1832, and the south end was realigned when the railway was constructed in 1873. Known as The Long Bridge, it was administered for over 700 years by a Trust who maintained it, toll-free, until 1961 when the local Highways Department took over.

|| Cross the bridge and take the second on the left which is Boutport
|| Street. Bear left by the Hearts of Oak pub into High Street, and right
|| into a narrow cobbled alley, Church Lane.

Along here is a school built for 'Twenty poor maids, founded by Alice Horwood in 1659.' Around the corner are almshouses with the upper storeys leaning outwards quite alarmingly.

|| Walk straight across the next junction of the paths, across Butchers
|| Row, through the Pannier Market, across Joy Street and bear right
|| alongside the new Green Lane buildings, turning left at the end
|| back into Boutport Street.

On the left is St. Peter's, the parish church, whilst on the right, to the right of the road is a church hall, and to the left, St. Anne's Chapel. This was endowed as a chantry in 1459, and became a grammar school at the Dissolution, staying thus until 1908. One alumnus was the poet John Gay. Between 1685 and 1785, the Heugenot's used the building as a place of worship. It is now a museum of the history of schooling, open in the summer, Tuesdays to Saturdays only.

Looking along Butchers Row, there are elegantly symetrical open shop fronts displaying meat and fish. How long the EC killjoys will allow this delightfully quaint state of affairs to last is open to debate. The white building at the end on the right is the Guildhall, built in 1826 in the Grecian style.

The Pannier Market was built in 1855, and is a wonderful example of a Devonian covered market.

|| Walk along here, bearing left into Mermaid Walk, past the North
|| Country Pub – selling south country (Usher's) beer – and to an
|| island. Cross the road, walk over the bridge and 50 yards along on
|| the right is a cycleway. This leads to a high embankment alongside
|| the river and follows it in a semi-circle before reaching a wall. A
|| sharp left here brings the walk to a road. Turn right and
|| immediately left past The Reform Inn and into Pilton Street. Pass
|| The Chichester Arms to the top of the street, turning left by the
|| almshouses.

Pilton is a place of real antiquity. Once the major settlement, Barnstaple had overtaken it by Domesday, leaving the village now very much a suburb of the market town. On the hill here, around 880, King Alfred built a *burh*, one of only four in Devon. These were fortified places for defence against marauding Danes. In 893, it was a vital part of the English defences as about 40 ships besieged the area, a further hundred attacking Exeter to the south. Alfred rushed reinforcements westwards, but the Danes retreated before battle could be joined. Pilton had done its job.

The Priory was one of the earliest establishments to be affected by non-conformist feelings; swept away in 1536. By then, it was already in terminal decline, having only three occupants. It was a cell of Malmesbury Abbey, founded during the 12th century. The site was to the north of St Mary the Virgin. This was originally the priory church, built around 1320 and has some very handsome work inside. There are two screens of great antiquity, and the tester over the font is unusual and ornate.

An indication of the importance of Pilton in earlier times can be found in records of the Wool Tax. In 1394, the town was producing more wool than Exeter. The main street is a charming hotchpotch of styles and vintages; the sort of place that is full of character and will probably never happen again. It's a sobering thought that much of the aesthetic attraction of these places existed before town planners exercised their malign influence over proposals to construct anything the slightest bit out of the ordinary. Character so often comes from what these people would call untidiness.

Continue along Under Minnow Road, past The Windsor Arms and follow the lane for just over half a mile, past Lions Mill and the first Public Footpath sign. At the crest of the next hill on the left is another sign pointing towards a stile to the right of a white house – Sunnyview. Into the field, head towards the left, through a gate in the far right corner, and pass a copse on your left before heading towards a gate to the right of some farm buildings. Through this gate, turn left, and after a few yards, the lane drops down into the farmyard. Here, keep right. There is a telephone pole just to the right, and beyond, four trees. Stand by the pole and aim for the second tree on the right. Walk in a straight line past the tree, and the next stile is beyond. Through there, follow the track along the contour and through a gate into an unmade road and into Ashford.

Ashford is a tiny hillside village, the centre of which is entirely unaffected by the holiday area surrounding; caravan sites, and everything associated with them. The views over the Taw estuary are quite superb with expanses of sand flats at low tide. The church of St. Peter is the only building of note in the village. This was completely rebuilt in Victorian times, much of it appearing to be a copy in miniature of SS Peter and Paul in Barnstaple. As befits its ancestry, much of the interior is plain, although there is a remarkable 14th century sculpture of St. John to be found in the vestry.

Turn right at the end of this lane, and right again up the hill towards the church. Fork left by this building and left by The Old Rectory. A Public Footpath sign points the way, alongside signs to Glebe House and By Ways. This narrow fenced path winds between the houses onto a lane. Turn left and at the end the path is to the right hand side of a garage. 20 yards down, a stile to the right leads across the top of two gardens to another stile.

Cross this one, and walk through a gateway, past the linhay (cowshed) and immediately turn right at a Waymarked gate. Within a few yards, another Waymarked gate takes the walk to the left. Straight ahead now, over two stiles close together, through two fields, to the lane and turn left. The Taw estuary is laid out below in all its splendour.

On reaching the busy main road turn right and cross. After a few yards, a track leads to the estuary, and immediately across a bridge over the old railway line, now The Tarka Trail and South West Coastal Path. A stile on the right gives access to the track bed, turn right, under the bridge. This offers a very pleasant easy walk back towards Barnstaple.

Past the rear of Pottington Industrial Estate – not as unpleasant as it may sound – and the posts of Barnstaple Rugby Club reach for the sky. Here, beyond a gate, the track bears left, and is well signposted into Mill Road. Along this road, a sign directs you right up an unnamed short narrow street, over a ramp to the river Yeo. Turn left, along Rolle Quay. This was once a railway siding, but extensive work in 1987 turned it into an attractive area with parking spaces. At the end of the quay, turn right over the bridge and right again, towards the tall new building.

On the left is a high mound where a motte and bailey castle once stood. Its history is somewhat obscure, with the possibility of there being some structure there before the Normans arrived. The first definitive records date it to the reign of Henry I.

‖ Carry on down North Walk, and where the road bears left, and
‖ straight on into a car park until you reach the sea wall. Turn left
‖ and approach the rear of Platform One restaurant.

This is so-called because it uses the buildings of the old Barnstaple Town
station. The narrow gauge Lynton and Barnstaple Railway terminated here,
where it met the standard gauge line. That opened on 11 May 1898, bringing
instant popularity (and wealth) to Lynton, previously well off the beaten
track. It was riotously popular in the summer, but struggled throughout the
winter. The line crossed the most spectacular terrain to the west of Exmoor,
climbing to a thousand feet at its summit. Eventually, the harsh realities
caught up and its owners, The Southern Railway, who had inherited the line
at the 1923 Grouping, closed it on 29 September 1935.

But its spirit lives on. There is a preservation group who hope to restore
some of the line, the signal cabin at the end of the platform being used by this
group. A section of the old track-bed at Parracombe is owned by a man who
operates a scale-model railway which is open during the summer, and
modellers throughout the country use this, one of the most fascinating
railways in the country, as their prototype.

‖ At the end of the short ramp past the signal cabin, turn right to
‖ regain the waterfront and then turn left.

Barnstaple was one of four Domesday boroughs of Devon. It was a
considerable port before the Taw began to silt up. Five ships to fight the
Armada were equipped here, on Great Quay; the *Dudley*, the *Tiger*, the *John
of Barnstaple*, the *Unicorn* and the *Prudex*. Today, nothing can reach the quay
save an occasional visit on the highest tides from the Lundy ferry *MS
Oldenberg*, chartered by local groups for an esturial cruise.

To the left, Merchants Exchange, built between 1708 and 1713, the open
portico known as Queen Anne's Walk. The colonnade was rebuilt in 1798.
The carvings here are exquisite.

‖ Continue alongside the water, pass under the road bridge, and
‖ take the flight of steps immediately to the left. This leads up
‖ alongside the Museum of North Devon – well worth a visit – to the
‖ main road. Turn hard left, back over the bridge and to the station.